PEDAGOGY & PRACTICE
FOR ONLINE
ENGLISH LANGUAGE
TEACHER EDUCATION

FARIDAH PAWAN

KELLY A. WIECHART

AMBER N. WARREN

JAEHAN PARK

This book has a
companion website. Go to
www.tesol.org/pedagogy
for additional resources.

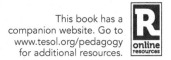

www.tesol.org/bookstore

TESOL International Association
1925 Ballenger Avenue
Alexandria, Virginia 22314 USA
Tel 703-836-0774 • Fax 703-836-7864
www.tesol.org

Director of Publishing: Myrna Jacobs
Cover Design: Citrine Sky Design
Copyeditor: Elizabeth Pontiff
Layout and Design: Capitol Communications, LLC
Printer: Gasch Printing, LLC

ISBN 9781942799139
Library of Congress Control Number 2016930005

Contents

Preface

We wrote this book in response to the trend toward online language teacher education and language teaching. An increasing number of college level programs are fully online (Allen & Seaman, 2010), and across the globe, more than 40 university-based teaching English to speakers of other languages (TESOL) master's-level programs are taught online (England, 2012). By some figures, as many as 50% of college students, which includes preservice and in-service teachers, may be enrolled in at least one online course by 2014 (Christensen, Horn, Caldera, & Soares, 2011).

In U.S. K–12 teacher education and professional development, there has been a greater focus on teacher evaluations since the No Child Left Behind Act of 2001 (Darling-Hammond & Richardson, 2009). To ensure that teachers perform well on these evaluations, school districts have increasingly turned to online teacher education and professional development (Kleiman, 2004; Dede, 2006). This shift demonstrates a recognition of the cost efficiency of online courses; underscores the fact that online teacher education is a way to eliminate access barriers (Reeves & Pedulla, 2011; Reeves & Li, 2012); and provides just-in-time, ongoing, and embedded support for busy teachers (Dede, Ketelhut, Whitehouse, Breit, & McCloskey, 2009). Evidence suggests that online courses can be effective in improving teacher knowledge, instructional practices, and student achievement (Dede et al., 2009; O'Dwyer et al., 2010).

However, while online coursework for professional development has lately increased in popularity, both researchers and educators lament the lack of focus on pedagogical training for online instructors. It remains an area in need of more rigorous attention (Dede, 2006; Dede et al., 2009). We strongly believe that pedagogy, rather than technology, should drive online instruction.

Our purpose in writing this book is thus twofold: (1) to discuss foundational theories of pedagogy and (2) to link those theories with our own practices in online courses in language teacher education and language teaching. Garrison, Anderson and Archer's (2001) social, cognitive, and teaching presences guide the pedagogical perspectives we assume and the practices we undertake to achieve the book's objectives. These presences are essential for learning by means of the online medium, and instruction through the medium should strive toward their attainment.

FIGURE P.1. COMMUNITY OF INQUIRY

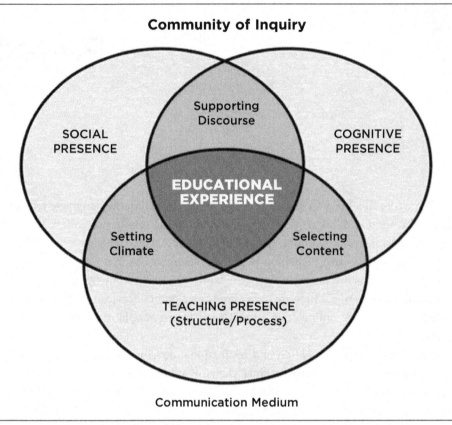

Community of Inquiry

From "Critical Inquiry in a Text-Based Environment: Computer Conferencing in Higher Education" by D. R. Garrison, T. Anderson, and W. Archer, 1999, *The Internet and Higher Education 2*(2–3), p. 88. Copyright 1999 by D. R. Garrison, T. Anderson, and W. Archer. Used with permission.

Each of the presences overlap but can be defined separately as well (Figure P.1). Social presence emerges from connections and relationships among participants in the classroom that lead to the development of a classroom community; cognitive presence is the intellectual challenge and sense of inquiry as participants engage in collaborative and reflective exploration, construction, integration, interrogation, and validation of ideas; and teaching presence is the instructor's course design, facilitation, and direct instruction in the online classroom that enable and enact the social and cognitive presences.

Similarly, the presences individually and jointly underlie the book's nine chapters, each of which begins with theoretical and conceptual frameworks that situate the online instructional practices that follow. The book thus describes teaching presence in online discussions (Chapter 1) and the concept of and ways to incorporate reflective teaching in online classrooms (Chapter 2). Chapter 3 covers universal design for learning (UDL) and how its principles apply in an intensive online workshop helping preservice teachers be inclusive in their instruction of diverse learners. We also discuss connectivism and how it underlies pre- and in-service teachers' use of online professional learning networks (PLNs) to learn, to sustain their expertise, and to seek support (Chapter 4), as well as active learning and just-in-time teaching (JiTT) in a hybrid and flipped doctoral seminar that blends the capacities of face-to-face and online media to support, reinforce, and extend learning (Chapter 5). We examine dialectical teaching and how it underlies the use of synchronous meetings to provide students in an online course with opportunities for interactive and practical discussions of case study projects to situate the projects within students' own contexts (Chapter 6), and hard and soft scaffolding in a process writing project in an online class demonstrating how instructors can build in as well as provide immediate support to students (Chapter 7). Chapter 8 discusses third spaces afforded by the online medium and utilized by instructors to provide a combination of intimacy, safe distance and a shared reality to guide students in discussing substantive cross-cultural issues. We conclude the book by describing a "future" that is a lived reality by trans-classroom teachers in which they are both face-to-face and online instructors (Chapter 9). We have included a glossary of terms, as well as a list of the applications and software mentioned in this book. Additionally, when you see **R**, go to this book's companion website, www.tesol.org /pedagogy, to download discussion questions and other helpful resources.

In writing this book, we are showcasing our pedagogy and practice that underlie our instruction of online courses. In doing so, we hope not only to guide but also to "de-mythify" online instruction to those who may be considering teaching using the medium. Hence, we refer in the first (Chapter 1) and in the final chapter (Chapter 9) to the wizard behind a curtain in the U.S. movie *The Wizard of Oz*. Toward the end of the movie, when Dorothy and her friends, the Scarecrow, the Tin Man, and the Cowardly Lion, have completed the task set for them by the wizard, when the curtain was lifted, it became apparent that there was only an ordinary man behind it who was adept at using the tools at his disposable to convince others to achieve what they believed was impossible. Similarly, by writing this book, we are lifting the curtain off online teaching as an encouragement and invitation for others considering teaching in the medium. We would like for readers to know that the online medium has provided us opportunities to explore new exciting possibilities in teaching and learning. It is evident to us as online instructors, that online teaching is enhanced by technology but not subsumed by it.

References

Allen, E., & Seaman, J. (2010). *Class differences: Online education in the United States.* Needham, MA: Sloan Consortium.

Bush, G. W. (2001, February). *No Child Left Behind*. Washington, DC: Department of Education, Office of the Secretary.

Christensen, C., Horn, M., Caldera, L., & Soares, L. (2011). *Disrupting college: How disruptive innovation can deliver quality and affordability to postsecondary education*. Mountain View, CA: Innosight Institute: Center for American Progress. Retrieved from http://www.americanprogress.org/issues/labor/report/2011/02 /08/9034/disrupting-college/

Darling-Hammond, L., & Richardson, N. (2009, February). Teacher learning: What matters? *Educational Leadership, 66*(5), 46–53.

Dede, C. (2006). *Online professional development for teachers: Emerging models and methods.* Cambridge, MA: Harvard Education Press.

Dede, C., Ketelhut, D. J., Whitehouse, P., Breit, L., & McCloskey, E. M. (2009). A research agenda for online teacher professional development. *Journal of Teacher Education, 60,* 8–19.

England, L. (Ed.). (2012). *Online language teacher education: TESOL perspectives.* New York, NY: Routledge.

Garrison, D. R., Anderson, T., & Archer, W. (1999). Critical inquiry in a text-based environment: Computer conferencing in higher education. *The Internet and Higher Education, 2*(2), 87–105.

Garrison, D. R., Anderson, T., & Archer, W. (2001). Critical thinking, cognitive presence, and computer conferencing in distance education. *American Journal of Distance Education, 15*(1), 7–23.

Kleiman, G. M. (2004, July). *Meeting the need for high quality teachers: E-learning solutions.* Paper presented at the U.S. Department of Education Secretary's No Child Left Behind Leadership Summit, Washington, DC. Retrieved from http://www.ed.gov/about/offices/list/os/technology/plan/2004/site/documents/Kleiman-MeetingtheNeed.pdf

No Child Left Behind Act of 2001, P.L. 107-110, 20 U.S.C. § 6319 (2002).

O'Dwyer, L. M., Masters, J., Dash, S. R., De Kramer, M., Humez, A., & Russell, M. (2010). Effects of on-line professional development on teachers and their students: Findings from four randomized trials. Chestnut Hill, MA: Technology and Assessment Study Collaborative. Retrieved from http://www.bc.edu/research/intasc/PDF/EFE_Findings2010_Report.pdf

Reeves, T. D., & Li, Z. (2012). Teachers' technological readiness for online professional development: evidence from the U.S. e-Learning for Educators initiative. *Journal of Education for Teaching: International Research and Pedagogy, 38,* 389–406.

Reeves, T. D., & Pedulla, J. J. (2011). Predictors of teacher satisfaction with online professional development: Evidence from the USA's e-Learning for Educators initiative. *Professional Development in Education, 37,* 591–611.

CHAPTER 1

Teaching Presence in Online Teaching

Faridah Pawan

[If we accept] successful teaching is a combination of intellectual commitment and embodied experience—that it is as much thought as it is action—then we need to advocate for the learning environment that allows both to play out.

—Lucia Volk, "Teach It Like You Mean It," 2012, para 23

In the U.S. movie *The Wizard of Oz*, a teenager named Dorothy along with her dog, Toto, are carried by a tornado to the Land of Oz. The movie goes on to describe Dorothy's quest to meet a well-known wizard to get his help to find her way home. She is accompanied by a group of three friends on her journey, namely the Scarecrow, the Tin Man, and the Lion. The Scarecrow wants the wizard to give him a brain so he can be intelligent; the Tin Man wants a heart so he can feel emotion; and the Lion wants courage so he can be brave. Although no one has ever seen the wizard, they are all convinced he has the power to help them. Part of their quest involves following a yellow brick road. The movie ends with Dorothy and her friends realizing that it is not the wizard himself but the knowledge of him being present that enables them to discover their own strengths and help themselves. This realization comes about when they find out that wizard is an ordinary man creatively using tools at his disposal to make things happen. In a way, the story of the Wizard of Oz represents the potential of presence to be a powerful guiding force to productive outcomes. However, there is careful planning and work behind the presence that makes it effective.

In this chapter, I discuss the theoretical conceptualization of teaching presence and provide examples of its implementation from an online graduate program for new and in-service teachers of English as a second language (ESL).

Presence Theory

Presence as a theoretical concept emerged from social presence and teacher immediacy research (Lowenthal & Parscal, 2008). Social presence is defined by Short, Williams, and Christie (1976) as the "saliency" or mutual noticeability of interlocutors, or communicators, and the consequences of that noticeability. The medium of communication is central to this conceptualization of saliency in that it determines the nature of the presence (Lowenthal & Parscal, 2008). For example in video materials, there is both visual and audio presence whereas in audio-only materials there is only audio presence. Immediacy is another component of social presence, which in its positive sense, Mehrabian and Epstein (1972) define as linguistic and nonlinguistic communication that develops a sense of affinity between communicators. It is the ability to effectively project approachability, likeability, and interest in sustaining engagement into the communication situation while being aware of these attributes in others.

Saliency and immediacy thus constitute social presence in that it depends on interlocutors' engagement with others around them. In this regard, social presence is "a complex and nuanced aspect of teaching" not a "checklist of behaviors, dispositions, measures, and standards" (Rogers & Raider-Roth, 2006, p. 265) as it is often simplistically regarded in an education climate of quantifiable accountability. Social presence thus requires teachers' critical self-awareness and capability to develop relationships and construct safe and trusting environments so that learning can take place. Thus, this conceptualization of social presence can be seen as foundational to the concept of presence in teaching, which according to Rogers & Raider-Roth, 2006, p. 267) has three aspects: connection to self, connection to students, and connection to subject matter and pedagogical knowledge. Each of these aspects is described below.

Connection to Self

To be invested in all that teaching involves, Rogers and colleagues (2006) assert that teachers must experience teaching as a projection of themselves as both an individual and a professional. Their identity, experiences, backgrounds, expertise, trust in their abilities, values, and morality influence the infrastructure and climate and nurture relationships they create in their classrooms. If authentic self-projection is constrained by externally imposed policies and requirements, teachers are likely to experience tentativeness and anxiety, and their teaching will become "emotionally flat and routinized" (Talbert, McLaughlin, & Rowan, 1993, p. 53). The principle of authentic self-projection holds true in online teaching. To achieve authentic self-projection online, teachers need to express themselves, their thinking, and their ways of doing things. They also need to communicate their grand design for a course (Anderson et al., 2001), which is reflective of who they are as teachers and as individuals.

Connection to Students

Rogers & Raider-Roth's (2006) relational stance is a view that emphasizes a psychological connection in which learning takes place in relationship to others. In the classroom, teachers who assume this stance emphasize relationship building, both between teachers and their students and among students as members of the classroom community. Rogers et al. emphasize the centrality of trust, empathy, authenticity and intersubjectivity (the ability to assume the viewpoints of others) in this stance, which allows for "expression, reciprocal appreciation of intentions and active work together" (p. 275) toward achieving meaningful ends. In this regard, teachers cannot cause learning but they can be influential in making it happen through the relationships they develop with students and through the materials and structures they put into place to support the relationships. As Johnson (2006) argue, teachers are in a "relationship of influence with students," a far more complex and deep relationship than the behavioristic "causal relationship" (p. 245) so often associated with two-dimensional views of teachers and teaching.

Connection to Subject Matter and Pedagogical Knowledge

To achieve a strong pedagogical connection, teachers need in-depth knowledge of their subject matter, the mastery of which will free them to focus on what students are doing with that subject matter (Dewey, cited in Rogers & Raider-Roth, 2006, p. 280) and to respond to students' questions and need for support in a timely and informed manner. Teachers need to maintain a feedback loop that involves taking action, assessing students' responses, and using these responses to shape the next steps. Another important component of the pedagogical connection is teachers' understanding of the process of knowing the subject matter (for example, knowing not only the Pythagorean theorem and its logic but also how Pythagoras came to its conceptualization). This level of understanding is necessary for teachers to gain insight into students' thinking so they can adjust their curriculum and lesson planning to promote students' understanding. Finally, teachers also need full understanding of the context of the school and schooling (Freeman & Johnson, 1998) in which their teaching takes place to make decisions within a realistic framework. The pedagogical connection aligns with Shulman's (1987) concept of teachers' expertise consisting of both content knowledge and pedagogical content knowledge. Parallels are also evident between Rogers' three types of teacher connection (i.e., to content, to the process of learning, and to the context) and Anderson et al.'s (2001) three categories of teaching presence: design and administration of content, facilitation and support of students' learning, direct instruction and intellectual leadership within instructional and institutional contexts (Table 1.1). The nature of teaching presence and its instructional manifestations in an online environment is the central of this chapter and they are discussed in the sections below.

Teacher Presence and Teaching Presence: A Difference with Pedagogical Significance

Anderson, Rourke, Garrison, and Archer (2001), who developed the idea of teaching presence, likened online teachers to one room schoolhouse teachers in North America in the days of yore. These teachers were responsible for managing all aspects of their classroom, from firing up the woodstove in the winter or opening windows in the summer to providing appropriate instruction for multiage and multilevel students. Today, while the specific tasks might be different, like their one room schoolhouse predecessors, teachers of online courses still need to maintain an environment conducive to learning and provide instruction that meets the needs of students from a wide range of backgrounds and levels of experience.

Anderson et al. (2001) wanted to understand the teacher's roles and their significance to students' learning in the online medium, which led them to construct the idea of teaching presence. They define teaching presence as "the design, facilitation and direction of cognitive and social processes for the purpose of realizing personally meaningful and educationally worthwhile learning outcomes" (p. 5; Table 1.1). In this conceptualization, the comprehensive notion of teaching presence also includes teacher presence or "direct instruction" by teachers in leading classroom learning using their expertise and "greater content knowledge" (Anderson et al., 2001, p. 8). In other words, teachers being present in the classroom is only one part of teaching presence.

I explored teaching presence in two studies of online classes (Pawan, Paulus, Yalcin, & Chang, 2003; Pawan, Yalcin, & Kuo, 2008). The first study focused on the types of teaching configurations in three online classrooms that led students to higher levels of thinking (integration, synthesis and resolution). The second focuses on the outcomes of teaching interventions in an online class to increase the effect of teaching presence on students' critical thinking.

In the first study, my colleagues and I found that teaching presence engaged students in higher levels of inquiry through presence that consisted of instructors' effective design and modeling of expected engagements; through their active, timely and regular participation in discussions; and finally through instructors' critical inquiry into and questioning of intellectually challenging issues in discussions. We researched three online language teacher education courses of different topics (literature in language teaching, the teaching of reading skills and technology integration into language teaching). We focused on instructional design as well as analysis of, using Garrison, Anderson and Archer's (2001) practical inquiry model (PIM), the daily postings of instructors and students at certain points in a semester for each of the classes. PIM outlines four phases of higher order thinking (triggering, exploration, integration and resolution), which were evident in online postings and thus enabled us to track and code postings at those phases. (I will refer to PIM in Chapter 2 as it is also relevant in guiding reflective teaching online.) Table 1.2 shows the specific weeks when postings were retrieved; the units of analysis, which consisted of coded postings; and the percentages comparing the number of coded postings for each phase in relation to the overall total of 229 coded posting units. Our findings confirmed that, overall, without overt instructor presence, students were engaged at the beginning levels of inquiry, namely at the exploration level 66% of the time, during which they mostly brainstormed and shared personal narratives, descriptions, and facts. (See Table 1.2, Phase 2.) There were negligible attempts by students to analyze, integrate the positions of others, or critically justify their own or others' positions, which represent the higher levels of integration and resolution/synthesis. However, in Technology in

TABLE 1.1. TEACHERS' ROLES IN ONLINE TEACHING

Design and Administration: Thinking through the process, structure, evaluation and components of the course	Facilitating Discourse: Supporting and encouraging participation toward the attainment of learning objectives	Direct Instruction: Providing intellectual and scholarly leadership
1. Build curriculum 2. Customize (repurpose) materials (include online commentaries, personal insights) 3. Design and administer mix of group and individual activities 4. Set and negotiate timelines 5. Provide guidelines and tips 6. Model appropriate netiquette 7. Model effective use of medium 8. Provide sense of "grand design" for course (narrative paths could be used to make explicit and implicit learning goals apparent)	1. Comment upon and encourage student responses 2. Draw in less active participants 3. Curtail effusive/ dominating comments 4. Help students find congruent links between opinions 5. Assess efficacy of discussion process	1. Present content 2. Initiate questions 3. Focus attention by directing attention to concepts 4. Confirm understanding through assessment and timely feedback 5. Diagnose and address misconceptions 6. Refer students to resources

Adapted from "Assessing Teaching Presence in a Computer Conferencing Context," by T. Anderson, L. Rourke, D. R. Garrison, and W. Archer, 2001, *Journal of Asynchronous Learning Networks, 5*(2) p. 1–17.

Language Teaching class, where the instructor had overt teaching presence by putting into place and actively using a participation structure of well-defined discussant roles (starter, provocateur, wrapper), there were more integrative and critical thinking questions posed, demonstrating the utility of a well-articulated design and transparent structure.

The results of the 2003 (Pawan et al.) study confirmed Garrison, Anderson, and Archer's (2001) assertion that "often students will be more comfortable remaining in a continuous exploration mode; therefore teaching presence is essential in moving the process to more-advanced stages of critical thinking and cognitive development" (p. 10). In particular, they state that the integration phase, in which students attempt to incorporate the views of others and to use them as a foundation to further develop their ideas, "requires active teaching presence to diagnose misconceptions, to provide probing questions, comments, and additional information in an effort to ensure continuing development, and to model the critical thinking process" (p. 10). In 2008 (Pawan et al.),

TABLE 1.2. ENGAGEMENT PATTERNS FROM THE PAWAN ET AL. 2003 STUDY

Class	Week	# Units	Phase 1 Trigger		Phase 2 Explor-ation		Phase 3 Inte-gration		Phase 4 Reso-lution		Off-Task	
			n	%	*n*	%	*n*	%	*n*	%	*n*	%
Literature-based Instruction	13–14	22	7	32	6	27	0	0	0	0	9	41
	15–16	18	4	22	10	56	3	17	0	0	1	6
Critical Reading Skills	6	47	2	4	39	83	1	2	0	0	5	11
	8	62	6	10	54	87	1	2	0	0	1	2
Technology in Language Teaching	5	37	3	8	21	57	12	32	0	0	1	3
	9	43	4	9	22	51	8	19	0	0	9	21
Total		229	26	11	152	66	25	11	0	0	26	11

From "Online learning: Patterns of engagement and interaction among in-service teachers," by F. Pawan, T. M. Paulus, S. Yalcin, and C. F. Chang, 2003, *Language Learning and Technology, 7*(3), p. 126. Used with permission.

we undertook an in-depth study of the role-based student participation design and format used in the Technology Integration class that proved effective in the 2003 study. We used the design and format as a teaching presence intervention and found that they were effective in increasing engagement at PIM's higher order thinking phases of synthesis and resolution but only up to a point. This was because student variables also impacted student engagement.

In the case of students' limited experiences with the subject matter (language teaching in this case), despite instructors' efforts to guide students engagement through the discussion roles, to push their questioning and engagement to a higher level of inquiry, students in that situation were most engaged in asking one-way directional questions that sought clarification at the exploration phase. This finding converges with prior research showing that novice learners tend to ask more questions on easier material (see Miyaki & Norman, 1978). Also, students who had limited experiences with online course partici-pation, were used to fixed rather than flexible time formats, or preferred the immediacy of engagement in face-to-face classrooms had issues of timeliness and frequency of participation. Without the pressure of regular engagement in a scheduled course, they often procrastinated in providing their responses and missed the teacher modeling. More often than not, these students would post at the end of the week, too late to be part of the engagement and feedback cycle, and in many cases, their postings were not read at all. Quality of posts was also an issue as, being aware of the situation; these students posted many rhetorical questions that did not require responses.

Another issue is that some students are less open to group work and critical discussion than others. We found that some participants were unwilling to expose themselves to peers whom they perceived as more online savvy or professionally experienced, an issue of "face" or self-protection. In several cases, we saw that students who kept to themselves were those who expressed an aversion to group work or were used to less contentious ways of engagement and sought to avoid the tension they experienced when they asked or were asked to justify positions. One student's statement illustrates such a perspective:

> As someone who tends to resist group work, I think that computers offer me anonymity, and I am probably more likely to make a comment in an atmosphere when I could not be openly ridiculed.

The indication that this student felt threatened by discussion involving counter-challenges to opinions points out the importance of learning style. There is no one-size-fits-all pedagogical approach, a principle that applies to all instructional settings. As Duffy et al. (1998) have noted, students can learn without being "quick and bold on their feet" (p. 63) in collaborative engagement. Thus, this study shows that the effectiveness of the teaching presence intervention through role assignments was moderated by students' variables.

Pathways of Practice: Developing Teaching Presence

The concept of presence in teaching has not often been taught in teacher education programs (Liston, 1995), largely because it is difficult to define and concretely demonstrate. However, the online environment provides facilities to trace and archive teaching moves through textual and multimodal means. My coauthors and I have taken advantage of those facilities in our teacher education program for English as a foreign language/English as a second language (EFL/ESL) teachers who are taking online classes to pursue licensing and certification.

Teaching presence as articulated by Anderson et al. (2001)—comprising course design and administration, facilitating discourse, and direct instruction—is the foundation for training sessions for instructors of the classes I supervise. I am informed by prior research, including the Pawan et al. (2003) and Pawan et al. (2008) studies described above, as well as instructional experiences. Below are a few examples of the teaching presence guidance I provide to instructors of online classes under my supervision.

Instructor Modeling and Timing of Participation

To make their grand design for a course apparent to students, instructors must clarify the planning of engagement and participation to themselves and make sure it is referenced throughout class discussions. If engaging students at the higher levels of thinking is what instructors want, they must make visible the various phases of engagement and questioning, such as those in the PIM model, that will lead students there. More important, instructors must model asking questions at those phases. For example, instead of asking,

"What do you think of semantic webbing," which might produce a simple valuative response (e.g., "I like it."), instructors ask more defined, inquiry-based questions such as, "What are the connections, contradictions, and surprises that you see in the concept of semantic webbing?" In this way, students are scaffolded and encouraged to think about issues from multiple perspectives so as to arrive at a more nuanced evaluation.

In addition to articulating their expectations of students, instructors should also clearly articulate how they will participate at regular, predetermined times throughout the week and how they will play a visible role in guiding students. For example, instructors could indicate that they will actively participate at the beginning and middle of weekly discussions and respond individually to at least one-third of the class membership each week.

The importance of continuously asserting this point to instructors is evident as shown in Table 1.2. Even in the Technology in Language Teaching class described above where the instructor's teaching presence positively impacted the quality of discussions at certain times of the semester, students continued to remain at the beginning levels of brainstorming and exploration for about 50% of the time. When asked about the situation, the instructor reported pulling back from continuously modeling higher order thinking questions to give room to students to push themselves onwards, a situation that seldom materialized. Accordingly, in the Literature in Language Teaching class, an undefined teaching presence produced lackluster student engagement. The instructor uploaded all the discussion questions for the course at the beginning and left it to the students to deal with them with little or no information about what his plans were to engage with students. His participation was unpredictable and uneven, which conveyed to the students that the instructor was not vested in the class nor in what they had to say. Such a situation contributed to students feeling disengaged and unmotivated to participate at higher levels of thinking.

The situation in both classes demonstrates that to move forward, students need effective teaching presence (articulated and transparent design, facilitation of discourse, and direct instruction). Lacking that presence, students' online discussions remain at the lower levels that appear "more like a series of declarations" (Connolly & Smith, 2000, p. 19) independent of each other and devoid of progress toward higher level thinking.

Role Definition and Self-Coding of Responses

Anderson et al. (2001) also suggest establishing teaching presence unobtrusively by modeling and assigning specific discussion roles to provide guidance while giving students responsibility and authority. These roles, such as starter, provocateur, and wrapper (discussed in detail in Chapter 2, "Reflective Pedagogy in Online Teaching") can focus the discussion and encourage student reflection. Both instructors and their students also need an array of role options to be able to choose those that align with their personalities and level of comfort. Appendix 1 lists a selection of roles provided by Curt Bonk, one of our colleagues in the Department of Instructional Systems and Technology at the Indiana University School of Education. These roles encourage others to share their thoughts meaningfully, to be accountable not just in the comments they make but also in the ways they connect with the views of others, and to find ways to share and critique intellectual and material resources. Without this guidance, students may find it difficult to initiate discussions, assume a perspective, and become relevant contributors. In online classes, novices to the medium are often seen making fly-by postings; that is, they flee after sharing their comments because they feel intimidated by the void or insecure about how their comments will be read and how they will be contextualized.

In that regard, I guide instructors to help their students self-code the discussion roles and types of postings they include in their discussions. This metacognitive strategy is based on the premise that awareness of the purpose and outcomes of collaborative interaction has educational value (Duffy, Dueber, & Hawley, 1998). The strategy encourages students to keep track of and reflect on how their responses relate to the collaborative learning objectives set by their instructors. Self-coding their own roles and responses may raise students' awareness, for example, of their participation in the four cyclical categories of postings in the practical inquiry model: trigger, exploration, integration, and resolution/synthesis. They can then title their postings accordingly, such as "Semantic Webbing: Integrating Responses Thus Far" or "Semantic Webbing: Exploring the Concept." Through these strategies, students remain in charge of their interactive behavior in discussions, and that may help them find purpose and a sense of investment in what they post.

Self-coding also includes students monitoring the length of their own postings, which could affect the quality of what they have to say and peer responses to postings. The frameworks my coauthors and I used in 2003 (Pawan et al.) and 2008 (Pawan et al.) studies demonstrated the importance of teaching presence. However, the frameworks did not allow us to articulate that we also saw that longer messages (300 words or more) did not necessarily result in higher quality postings. Frequently these lengthy postings did not incorporate issues raised by others or in the readings, indicating that students were not in a discussion mode but rather in a presentation mode when they wrote them. In addition there were fewer replies to extremely long messages compared to shorter messages, suggesting the longer messages were not being integrated into the flow of the discussion. I incorporate this information into instructor training as it reasserts the instructors' role to explicitly model for students their expectations, which in this case are appropriate self-coding as well as appropriate lengths in postings.

Making Puzzlement and Complexities Visible

Teaching presence includes direct instruction, which in its basic form is instructors' provision of content, readings, and resources. However, what is not often mentioned is that it also involves making visible the process of puzzlement, a process facilitated by the online medium and current technology. In training sessions, the instructors and I brainstorm about how this could be achieved. For example, we look to social media such as Twitter or blogs as places where we could make visible to students our questions and uncertainties as well as connections we are making as we read, in preparation for more structured and moderated discussions in our class discussion forums. Another effective approach to making the process visible is the creation of virtual discussion rooms for smaller groups to meet. Instructors can join one of the discussion groups and invite participants in other discussion groups to lurk and observe the types of questions, misconceptions, new issues, and so forth. This approach can be likened to the "fishbowl" approach to discussions, in which others observe and learn from conversations publicly conducted by peers.

I began teaching my first online in the fall semester of 2001. Because the class was for ESL and EFL teachers, the class consisted of individuals with varying experiences and national origins. Half the class was teachers from overseas, including the Middle East. The tragic events of September 11 took place in the third week of class and after that, there was total shutdown, meaning there were no postings in class for about a week and a half. I sensed that people feared their comments would be perceived as inadequate given the horrific circumstances or they would be challenged and ridiculed for their comments, given who they were and where they were from. During that entire time, I made visible and shared freely reactions at the national and state levels, as well as those of my colleagues and students on campus. I also made visible my own individual fears and struggles, several of which stem from the fact that I am not originally from the United States (Malaysian by birth), and I have Sanskrit-based first and last names. After a week I saw students coming back to class connecting with what I was sharing. Each week that semester we continued to bring forth what we were thinking and experiencing in the online space I created. The experience taught me that part of our effectiveness as online instructors consists of our ability to project ourselves and to be present as individuals as well as to help our students do the same. This includes sharing the complexities that make us human, which can provide a meaningful subtext for why we should stay together as members of a class.

Conclusion

Teaching presence encapsulates the roles of the teacher and the acts of teaching in an online environment. When effectively manifested, the online medium becomes a means for instructors and students alike to engage in critical thinking and meaningful engagement. Teaching presence in that regard is like the wizard whose presence led Dorothy and her three friends to take the perilous yellow brick road, a journey that enabled them to uncover the capabilities they had to help themselves.

R Questions for Further Discussion

1. What is your definition of teaching presence, and how does it differ from teacher presence, as described in the chapter?

2. Using a class you are familiar with as an example, how do you (or how does the instructor) establish teaching presence? Try to identify at least three aspects of the teacher's activity that constitute teaching presence and provide examples.

References

Anderson, T., Rourke, L., Garrison, R., & Archer, W. (2001). Assessing teaching presence in a computer conferencing context, *Journal of Asynchronous Learning Networks, 5*(2), 1–17.

Belenky, M. F., Clinchy, B. M., Goldberger, N. R., & Tarule, J. M. (1986). *Women's ways of knowing: The development of self, voice, and mind.* New York, NY: Basic Books.

Bonk, C. J. (2001). Role controversy: The 28 roles and 28 explanations of roles. Bloomington: Indiana University. Bloomington. Retrieved from http://www.indiana .edu/~bobweb/r546/modules/cooperative_learning/bob_handouts/28_roles _explanations.html

Connolly, B., & Smith, M. W. (2000). Teachers and students talk about talk: Class discussion and the way it should be. *Journal of Adolescent & Adult Literacy, 46*(1), 16–26.

Duffy, T. M., Dueber, B., & Hawley, C. L. (1998). Critical thinking in a distributed environment: A pedagogical base for design of conferencing systems. In C. J. Bonk & K. S. King (Eds.), *Electronic collaborators: Learner-centered technologies for literacy, apprenticeship, and discourse* (pp. 51–78). Mahwah, NJ: Lawrence Erlbaum Associates.

Freeman, D., & Johnson, K. E. (1998). Reconceptualizing the knowledge-base of language teacher education. *TESOL Quarterly, 32,* 397–417.

Garrison, D. R., Anderson, T., & Archer, W. (2001). Critical thinking, cognitive presence, and computer conferencing in distance education. *American Journal of Distance Education, 15*(1), 7–23.

Herring, S. C. (2003). Gender and power in online communication. In J. Holmes and M. Meyerhoff (Eds.), *The handbook of language and gender* (pp. 202–228). Oxford: Blackwell Publishers.

Johnson, K. E. (2006). The sociocultural turn and its challenges for second language teacher education. *TESOL Quarterly, 40*(1), 235–257.

Liston, D. P. (1995). Intellectual and institutional gaps in teacher education. In J. W. Garrison & A. G. Rud Jr. (Eds.), *The educational conversation: Closing the gap* (pp. 129–142). Albany, NY: SUNY Press.

Lowenthal, P. R., & Parscal, T. (2008). Teaching presence. *The Learning Curve, 3*(4), 1–4.

Mehrabian, A., & Epstein, N. (1972). A measure of emotional empathy. *Journal of Personality, 40*(4), 525–543.

Miyake, N., & Norman, D. A. (1978). *To ask a question, one must know enough to know what is not known.* (Report No. 7802.) San Diego, CA: California University, San Diego: Center for Human Information Processing. (ERIC Document Reproduction Service No. ED175883)

Pawan, F., Paulus, T. M., Yalcin, S., & Chang, C. F. (2003). Online learning: Patterns of engagement and interaction among in-service teachers. *Language Learning & Technology, 7*(3), 119–140.

Pawan, F., Yalcin, S. T., & Kuo, X. J. (2008). Teaching interventions and student factors in online collaboration. In B. Barber & F. Zhang (Eds.), *Handbook of research on computer enhanced language acquisition and learning* (pp. 406–423). Hershey, PA: IGI Global.

Rodgers, C. R., & Raider-Roth, M. B. (2006). Presence in teaching. *Teachers and Teaching: Theory and Practice, 12*(3), 265–287.

Short, J., Williams, E., & Christie, B. (1976). *The social psychology of telecommunications.* Hoboken, NJ: John Wiley & Sons.

Shulman, L. S. (1987). Knowledge and teaching: Foundations of the new reform. *Harvard Educational Review, 57*(1), 1–23.

Talbert, J., McLaughlin, M., & Rowan, B. (1993). Understanding context effects on secondary school teaching. *Teachers College Record, 95*(1), 35–68.

Volk, L. (2012). Teach it like you mean it. Washington, DC: National Education Association. Retrieved from http://www.nea.org/home/50447.htm

R Appendix 1.1

Adapted from "Role Controversy: The 28 Roles and 28 Explanations of Roles" by C. J. Bonk, 2001. Bloomington: Indiana University. Bloomington. Retrieved from http://www.indiana.edu/~bobweb/r546/modules/cooperative_learning/bob_handouts/28_roles_explanations.html. Used with permission.

Role Play Explanations

- Your job for this week is that of Reporter/Summarizer/Reviewer/Commentator: As a result, you can only summarize across, review, and comment on points made when addressing this problem.

- Your job for this week is that of Editor/Refiner/Perfecter/Improver. As a result, you can only edit, refine, perfect, and improve points made when addressing this problem.

- Your job for this week is that of Controller/Executive Director/CEO/Leader. As a result, you can only oversee the process, report overall findings and opinions, and try to control the flow when addressing this problem.

- Your job for this week is that of Connector/Relator/Linker/Synthesizer. As a result, you can only connect, interrelate, and link ideas made when addressing this problem.

- Your job for this week is that of Decider/Judge/Settler. As a result, you can only make decisions, evaluate, settle, and judge ideas when addressing this problem.

- Your job for this week is that of Devil's Advocate/Critic/Censor. As a result, you can only take opposite points of view for the sake of an argument and be an antagonist when addressing this problem.

- Your job for this week is that of Reflector/Thinker/Speculator/Observer/Watcher. As a result, you can only observe, watch, reflect, think meditate, and speculate on the discussion when addressing this problem.

- Your job for this week is that of Warrior/Debater/Arguer/Conqueror/Bloodletter. As a result, you can only take your ideas into action, debate with others, persist in your arguments and never surrender or compromise no matter what the casualties are when addressing this problem.

- Your job for this week is that of Idea Squelcher/Biased/Preconceiver. As a result, you can only squelch good *and* bad ideas of others and submit your own prejudiced or biased ideas when addressing this problem.

- Your job for this week is that of Slacker/Slough/Slug/Surfer Dude. As a result, you can only sit back quietly and listen, make others do all the work for you, and generally have a laid back attitude (e.g., go to the beach) when addressing this problem.

- Your job for this week is that of Artist/Idea Person/Visionary/Muse. As a result, you can only create; draw; and present proposals, alternatives, provocations, and new ideas when addressing this problem.

- Your job for this week is that of Planner/Predictor/Guesser/Flowcharter. As a result, you can only think ahead of the rest in a rational, logical, and structured way and then plan, predict, and guess where we should head or what we should do next when addressing this problem. As a result, you can only initiate and organize large scale change, flowchart possible growth patterns, and generate new ways for doing things when addressing this problem.

- Your job for this week is that of being Emotional/Sensitive/Intuitive. As a result, you can only be the fire and warmth of emotions, feelings, hunches, and intuitions when addressing this problem.

CHAPTER 2

Reflective Pedagogy in Online Teaching

Faridah Pawan

Experience is the starting point for teacher development, but in order for experience to play a productive role, it is necessary to examine such experience.

—*Richards and Lockhart, 1995, pp. 3-4*

In teacher education, reflective teaching has become the focus of efforts to bridge the gap between theory and practice and to value insider knowledge about teaching (Bailey, Curtis, & Nunan, 1998). Kyriacou (1994), for example, asserts that teachers are "the main agents of change of their own professional growth . . . in that teachers who regularly think of their own teaching are more likely to develop and improve their classroom practice" (p. 10). Freeman and Johnson (1998) point out that external information seldom replicates teachers' classroom experiences or contributes to their practical theory of teaching. Eylon (2000) defined the practical theory of teaching as a teacher's integrated theory for teaching that evolves from the day-to-day experiences of teaching and living in the classroom. Reflective teaching thus involves teachers' self-evaluation of their practical theory whereby they subject their personal beliefs about teaching and learning, as well as their teaching practices, to critical analysis.

Information from reflective teaching directly focuses teachers' attention on not only what is happening in their own classrooms but also who they are as teachers. This is a necessary practice as teaching occurs so quickly and intuitively that "much of what happens in the classroom is unknown to the teacher" (Richards & Lockhart, 1994, p. 3). Peck and Westgate (1994) argue that reflective teaching professionalizes teachers as, similar to other professionals, reflective teachers draw upon their accumulated experience and knowledge and "display judgment in using it" (p. 8) in classroom practice.

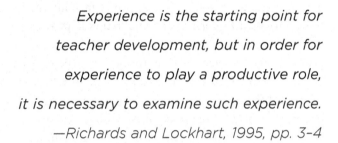

In this chapter, I focus on ways of incorporating the practice of reflective teaching in online teacher education classes for in-service teachers. I chose this focus because online classes have several inherent qualities, such as a textual basis and asynchronicity that provide unique opportunities for modeling and practicing reflective teaching.

Reflective Teaching as Pedagogy in the Online Medium: A Natural Convergence

Baran, Correia, and Thompson (2011) assert that it is often difficult for online teachers and teacher educators to find their teaching selves, that is, what defines them as teachers and what defines their instruction based on their knowledge as well as experiences. Without the communication cues that face-to-face interaction affords, teachers may find it hard to identify their leadership and facilitation approaches and ways to assess their effectiveness. However, the online platform, largely because of its textual basis and asynchronicity, provides its own effective ways for both instructors and learners to engage with each other and monitor their own performance through reflection. The advantage of asynchronicity, the time differential in an online discussion forum, is that it gives the individual the ability to connect, interact and think along with others independent of time and space.

Garrison (2003, p. 50) points out that communication in online settings "encourages if not requires reflection." Although visual, audio, and synchronous applications are readily available and frequently incorporated into online courses, Garrison (2007) points out that communications in online courses are more commonly undertaken textually and not in immediate time but at a time convenient for students. These textual and asynchronous facilities enable students to arrest and freeze their thoughts and ideas in stable artifacts that enable them to reexamine, question, deconstruct, and reformulate what they share online. These are the very qualities that led to writing being hailed, by literacists such as Walter Ong (1982) and Eric Havelock (1986), as a technical revolution that reversed the ephemerality of ideas and contributed to their greater precision.

Also, because asynchronous online writing allows space for deliberation that is possible only because others are not present (Ferris, 2002), it fosters deeper assessment of information through metacognition (Akyol & Garrison, 2011). Jacobs and Paris (1987) described metacognition as self-appraisal of cognition and self-management of thinking. The former refers to "the static assessment of what an individual knows about a given domain or task" and the latter to the "dynamic aspects of translating knowledge into action" (pp. 258–259). And, while metacognition is often regarded as a private, internal activity, Jacobs and Paris (1987) emphasize its social nature as

> knowledge about cognitive states or processes that can be shared between individuals. That is, knowledge about cognition can be demonstrated, communicated, examined, and discussed. Often, metacognition is exchanged verbally or used privately but, for us, the essential defining feature is that metacognition can be made public. Thus, it is reportable, conscious awareness about cognitive aspects of thinking. (p. 258)

As a metacognitive activity, reflection is also enhanced by connectivity with others. This connectivity is maximized by the interactivity of text-based online teaching. Metacognition is facilitated through collaborative tasks and discussion, an assertion that is reaffirmed by Garrison, Anderson, and Archer's (2000) community of inquiry framework, which loops learning through a cyclical process of private and public reflections (Figure 2.1). This cycle of construction, examination, reflection, and reconstruction of ideas is fundamental in online learning and teaching.

As pointed out by Ong (1982), writers claim ownership of their written ideas, which fosters a heightened level of consciousness of individual identity. The seriousness of plagiarism as academic misconduct is an indication of the uncompromising nature of this sense of ownership. Because of the high stakes of personal ownership of ideas, a high value is placed on not only the clarity but also the quality of ideas expressed, which can be more carefully crafted, substantive, and informed in online discussions than in spontaneous face-to-face communication. The caveat, however, is that this high quality depends

FIGURE 2.1. PRACTICAL INQUIRY MODEL

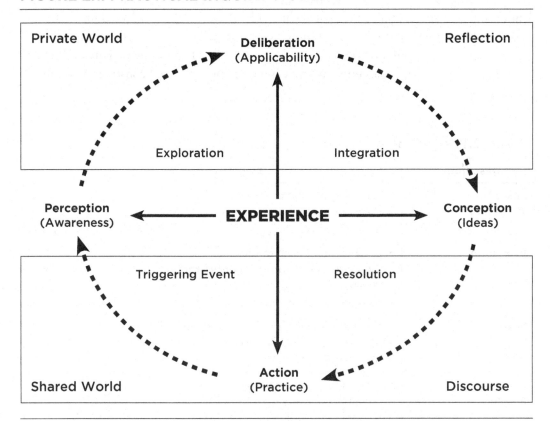

Note. From "Critical Inquiry in a Text-Based Environment: Computer Conferencing in Higher Education" by D. R. Garrison, T. Anderson, and W. Archer, 2000, The Internet and Higher Education, 2(2–3), p. 88. Copyright 2000 by D. R. Garrison, T. Anderson, and W. Archer. Used with permission.

on instructors' skillful structuring of class interactions and their own active and timely participation (see An, Shin, & Lim, 2009; Clark & Sampson, 2008; Kanuka, Rourke, & Laflamme, 2007; Pawan & Honeyford, 2009).

Practical Inquiry Model as a Foundation for Online Reflective Pedagogy

Online teaching as a field benefits from Garrison et al.'s (2000) conceptualization of the community of inquiry framework operationalized by the practical inquiry model (PIM; see Figure 2.1). The stages in the model provide helpful guidelines for implementing reflective pedagogy in online instruction. PIM is predicated on sustained reflective discourse through the cyclical stages of ideas being triggered, explored, integrated and resolved through vicarious and real-life application of understanding (Garrison, 2007, p. 65). Table 2.1 provides detailed explanations of the stages.

All these stages cycle to and from the private (individual reflections) and the public (collaborative reflections) domains of learning. This looping is facilitated by asynchronicity, which allows the individual to connect, interact, and think along with others independent of time and space, and connectivity, which allows for virtually unlimited interactions among multiple parties in multiple directions (Garrison, 2003). These properties are at the core of online teaching. As shown in Table 2.1, this freedom of interactivity allows for questioning, speculating, countering, complicating, synthesizing, and constructing on the way to problem solving.

TABLE 2.1. PRACTICAL INQUIRY MODEL: INDICATORS

Descriptors	Sample Indicators
Phase 1 Triggering	• Recognizing the problem • Sensing puzzlement
Phase 2 Exploration	• Diverging in opinions • Exchanging information • Sharing suggestions for consideration • Brainstorming • Leaping into conclusions
Phase 3 Integration	• Converging with others with tentative solutions • Connecting and synthesizing ideas • Creating solutions
Phase 4 Resolution	• Applying ideas vicariously • Testing solutions • Defending solutions

Note. From "Critical Inquiry in a Text-Based Environment: Computer Conferencing in Higher Education" by D. R. Garrison, T. Anderson, and W. Archer, 2000, *The Internet and Higher Education, 2*(2-3), p. 88.

PIM has its roots in the theoretical foundations of reflective pedagogy. Interest in this pedagogy emerged as a "grand idée" (Jay & Johnson, 2002, p. 73) because of demands for realistic and grounded professional development. The traditional approach in teacher education consists of the transfer of theoretical knowledge from experts to prospective and in-service teachers, through instruction and assignments, which the teachers are then expected to apply in their classrooms (Korthagen & Kessels, 1999; Korthagen, 2001; Korthagen, Loughran, & Russell, 2006). The problem with this approach is that it ignores the difference between theory and practice, so that teachers often cannot see the relevance of knowledge that is provided before they try to use it in practice, a problem known as "feed-forward" (Korthagen & Kessels, 1999, p. 6). In this situation, the meaningfulness of the information may elude learners who lack experiences in which to contextualize it, resulting in knowledge that is abstract, systemized, and generalized rather than concrete, flexible, and specific. Such disconnection of knowledge from real-life circumstances is a core criticism of second language acquisition theories that are especially prevalent in TESOL programs.

Elements of PIM can be traced to several models of reflective pedagogy, including the ALACT model of teacher reflection (ALACT is an acronym for the stages of reflection of action, looking back, awareness of essential aspects, creating alternative methods of action and trial; see Korthagen, 2001; Korthagen & Kessels, 1999). PIM's triggering, exploration, integration and resolution phases align with those in ALACT, which start with teachers identifying real-life teaching experiences as a trigger for reflection. This step is followed by looking back and becoming aware of the essential aspects of the experiences (similar to PIM's exploration) and then connecting those aspects with other experiences, their own or those of others (PIM's integration). ALACT's final phases, in which teachers come up with and test alternative methods, resonate with PIM's resolution stage. The outcome of both the ALACT and PIM models is teacher education that is realistic in the sense that it is grounded in teachers' practices while strengthening the link between practice and theory.

Nevertheless, critical reflection is not specifically articulated in either PIM or ALACT, although it is essential in reflective pedagogy models such as Van Manen's (1977). In Van Manen's three levels of reflectivity, critical reflection is the highest level, at which teachers question all aspects of the status quo as they reflect on issues of justice and equity in instruction. The first two levels are on the application of principles (technical rationality) and the clarification of assumptions that underlie teaching actions and goals (practical action). Nevertheless, though it is not specifically articulated in the ALACT and PIM models, the reflective interrogation of actions at the final stages of both models suggests that criticality and "problematizing the given" (Pennycook, 1999, p. 343) are part of the reflective processes at those advanced and complex levels.

In the following section, I discuss the "pathways of practice" (Pawan & Thomalla, 2005) in online teaching and the professional development of teachers of English as a second language informed and transformed by reflective teaching pedagogy.

Pathways of Practice: Reflective Teaching Pedagogy

Reflective pedagogy is central to both the teacher professional programs that I have directed in the past and those I currently provide leadership for. These include joint federally and state-funded master's level professional development programs to qualify English as a second language (ESL) and content area teachers (CATs) for ESL state licensure; programs for English as a foreign language/English as a second language (EFL/ESL) professionals leading to a certificate in teaching or teacher training; and the Master's International degree program in EFL/ESL for Peace Corps volunteers. I will describe these programs below as well as the implementation of reflective pedagogy in practice.

Although available in onsite and combined onsite and online tracks, all these programs have been offered primarily online. The reasons for offering the courses online converge with the reflective stance that I take as a teacher educator, as should be clear in the descriptions of each of the programs.

Tandem Certification Program for Indiana Teachers

The Tandem Certification program for Indiana Teachers (TACIT), a federally funded 5-year program, was initiated in the 2004–2005 school year to address the immediate training needs of the limited number of ESL-certified teachers (ESLT) in Indiana (with 1 ESLT per 80 English learners, ELs). Many of these ESLTs could not take time away from their classrooms to pursue professional development. This constraint, however, became an advantage in that it created an opportunity to provide an "embedded" program for teachers. Programs that do not remove teachers from their classrooms enable (a) sharing ideas and events that are grounded in the teachers' immediate experiences and (b) teachers and peers reflecting on and theorizing about teaching practice both as it is happening and after it takes place (individual and collaborative reflection in action and on action). This approach is aligned with reflective pedagogy in that theorizing about teaching begins with grounded practice and not the reverse. The goal of reflective pedagogy is to facilitate teachers' generation of their own theories of practice based on "understanding and developing a principled basis for their own classroom work" (Korthagen, 2001, p. 52). As Korthagen observes, reflection is the instrument that translates teachers' experiences into dynamic knowledge, "an ongoing process consisting of experience, looking back on experience, analysis and reorganization" (p. 52). Teachers' knowledge of the specifics of their own situation is used to help them achieve a realistic macro-level understanding of the teaching practices most relevant in their own settings.

An example of situated knowledge development was the assignment for each teacher to webcast one period of his or her classroom teaching to be observed and reflected upon by classmates at their convenience. As the teacher was teaching, he or she posted ongoing reflections (reflection in action) using whatever portable device was available (e.g., IPad, laptop computer, mobile phone). Teachers were able to upload their video clips onto Oncourse, Indiana University's virtual course management system used in the TACIT program. Afterwards, the teacher observed the archived webcast for individual reflection, posted the results, and later joined discussion of the teaching on the asynchronous forum with classmates and the instructor. Understanding and theorization of practice emerged from these individual and joint reflections.

Theorization of practice is a process by which teachers reflect upon and articulate their experiences using the discourse and vocabulary acquired in the course (Freeman 2002) in ways that align with their understanding of what is happening in their class-rooms. It also provides a macro perspective on their hypotheses to explain what they observe. On the basis of multiple inputs (during and after webcasts), the TACIT teachers then posted their theory of practice in the asynchronous forum to be commented upon and modified over time with additional information and awareness. An example of teacher theorization is as follows:

> Lots of meaningful comments here, so I'm going to focus on two aspects in self-assessment: motivation and training of learners. There is some evidence, right (you saw it?), that my students will be inherently more motivated if they're able to set their own learning goals and thus learn what they want to learn . . . but, putting that into practice becomes a bit muddier as you can see from what is happening in my class with the online LinguaFolio. Several of you mentioned one gap: training the learners. You saw how I underestimated the level of support that learners will need to utilize the folio. I am beginning to see that developing motivation, training learners and continuous scaffolding must be within the self-assessment, if not already.

The theorization stages are in tandem with those of Garrison, Anderson, and Archer's (2001) practical inquiry in online learning, in that teachers started with puzzling over triggering events (critical incidents and webcasted lessons) and exploring their implications alone and with others. The teachers then integrated all these ideas and proposed theory that could be tested for its relevance in the classroom vicariously or in actual practice (see Table 2.1).

Interdisciplinary Collaborative Program

The thrust of my job as the director of the Interdisciplinary Collaborative Program (ICP), a federally funded program for about 180 ESL and content area teachers (ESLTs and CATs) was to develop and sustain joint professional development programs for teachers from 25 school districts in Indiana. The program allowed ESLTs and CATs to learn from each other how to make their instruction accessible to ELs, making teacher collaboration an essential component. Because the teachers were distributed across the state, the online medium was the most accessible way to bring them together. However, such collaboration can be difficult to achieve. One of the issues most troubling to online instructors, includ-ing those in the ICP, has been the prevalence of "serial monologues" (Henri, 1991) in asynchronous discussion forums.

Serial monologues are discussions in which participants share reflections on teaching experiences and freely express their opinions with **minimal effort made to connect to** and integrate the contributions of others. In an evaluation study, Pawan, Paulus, Yalcin, and Chang (2003) concluded that most of the time, students restricted themselves to individual brainstorming and explorations rather than engaging in collaborative, reflective inquiries at the higher levels of learning. Among the problems uncovered in the study were that collaborative reflections were hindered by the online instructors' failure to always provide an appropriate task structure. Thus, to address the problems, students in ICP courses were assigned to one of three weekly moderating roles, previously mentioned in Chapter 1, that made them specifically responsible for drawing out reflections from and fostering collaboration with classmates. Following are brief illustrations of these roles as they were initially modeled for the class by the instructor.

> **Starter role.** On Monday, I [instructor] will be posting prompt 1. On Wednesday, you will post the second prompt early in the evening between 6 and 8 p.m. EST. Your prompt should arise out of the discussions that you see emerging up to that point as well something that you feel is essential to be discussed after you've reflected on classmates' contributions. Point out or draw out connections between classmates' ideas.

> **Provocateur role.** Throughout the week, you will weave in and out of discussions in your group, connecting classmates' ideas, pushing for clarification, pointing out contradictions, raising new/contrary ideas/resources, and so forth.

> **Wrapper role.** As a wrapper, you post the midweek wrap for each group under the first prompt by Wednesday evening and the week's wrap by Saturday. It is important that, in addition to summarizing and reflecting upon ideas and resources shared by colleagues, you also demonstrate how classmates' ideas have come together to push us to a new place of understanding as a class.

It was also important for online instructors in the ICP to regularly engage in reflective "self-storying" to provide students with a sense of the grand design of the course (Anderson, Rourke, Garrison, & Archer, 2001, p. 6). Following is an example of my own self-storying, which I shared with students:

> At this early point in the semester, I invite you all to share with me this week, through our individual and private emails, how things are going for you. I will share with you a little bit of where I am in the class. I would like first to say that I am extremely proud of all of you for hanging in there. For most of you, this is your first experience taking classes online, and it has been amazing for me to watch and see your efforts and perseverance to stay with and in the class. I also see collegiality and friendships not only through the sharing of your expertise but also through putting forth out there and responding compassionately and responsibly to each other's vulnerabilities, questions, and inquiries. I feel that we are becoming a community brought together by common interests, curiosity, and respect for each other's work.
>
> I will also share with you a few things that keep me awake at night. I worry when I see instances of us not responding to each other's comments but just going about posting our own ideas without acknowledging or taking into

consideration the views of others. The aim of the class, of course, is for us to build a knowledge base together. I worry about how much I should direct conversations or interject my views in the discussions when I see that happening. I work hard to find balance in my own participation so that you do not feel that I am taking over conversations. Let me know your thoughts about this.

In any case, I may have gone a bit too long with my own self-storying but I wanted to share with you some of what I am thinking as an invitation for you to reflect with me some of your thoughts.

It should be noted here also that regular communication at a more personal level not only allowed instructors to touch base with students on the overall goals of the class in an informal and nonthreatening manner but also provided an outlet for the phatic element, that is, the social presence (Anderson et al., 2001) and human dimension in online instruction. Such presence overlaps with teaching presence discussed in Chapter 1 in that it not only asserts instructors' leadership and guidance but, more importantly, creates an invitation for authentic participation and a sense of investment for both teachers and students to stay engaged and interested in the classroom.

EFL/ESL Professional Development Program via Distance Education

EFL/ESL Professional Development Program via Distance Education (EPDE) is an online certificate program for a special group of individuals, many of them U.S. in-service teachers in the United States or other countries and international professionals in their home countries who seek the latest information but lack funding or opportunities to pursue a complete master's program. Many of these individuals feel compelled to make an immediate difference given their understanding of the marginalization of ELs in the United States and the overwhelming demands placed on students (and their teachers) internationally to acquire English. Often EPDE participants are mature, currently employed, and busy individuals looking to move to a second and personally meaningful career. They approach coursework with great purpose and expect to be able to critically reflect upon their experiences as a basis for understanding.

To accommodate such students, online courses in the program follow Van Manen's (1977) reflectivity levels: technical reflection, practical action, and critical reflection. For technical reflection, the focus is on the efficiency of the application of educational knowledge and principles to the attainment of specified goals; for practical action, the goal is to clarify assumptions underlying teaching and assessment of the educational outcomes of instructional action (Zeichner & Liston, 1987); and finally, critical reflection targets the moral and ethical justifiability of educational practices, policies, and social infrastructures. Reflection at this level results in judgment situated in the social, historical, political, and cultural contexts in which teaching and learning are undertaken (Hatton & Smith, 1995). Another outcome of critical reflection is student advocacy, which is a central if not a critical component of ESL/EFL teachers' work (Athanases & Martin, 2006). According to Athanases and Martin (2006), teacher advocacy for English language learners involves "casting all aspects of school as problematic rather than given" (p. 628) and using expertise within oneself rather than merely relying on others to intercede on their students' behalf.

How are all these levels of reflection undertaken via distance education? There are of course multiple ways, including the use of synchronous and asynchronous platforms that have text, voice, and visual archival capabilities. For example, in one of the EPDE courses, participants are engaged in technical reflections on their tandem learning, in which participants teach each other a new language or a new skill online. Adobe Breeze, Skype, Google Hangout, and Voice Thread are used. Smartphone applications are useful when students are in different time zones as their voice quality is better and voice lags are minimal. Examples of such applications include KakaoTalk, HeyTell, Whatsapp, and Tango. Students' joint reflections usually yield information and ideas on how best to approach online instruction.

In another activity to move EPDE participants toward reflecting on the reasons for their teaching moves (Van Manen's practical action), they develop and reflect upon action mazes. These are interactive language learning dilemmas with multiple choices of actions and accompanying consequences for each. The participants identify real-life language teaching situations they have encountered as learners, parents, or teachers and use these as starting points in their action mazes. Quandary, freeware that is part of Half-Baked Software, has been used for this purpose. The application enables users to spontaneously generate multiple alternatives in their action mazes.

As mentioned earlier, EPDE participants are usually drawn to the program because of a social and personal mission to make a difference. Critical reflections on that sense of mission, which generally inform their application statements and merge academics with social responsibility, are thus an essential component of EPDE coursework. One of the ways in which critical reflection is undertaken is through critical incidents (CIs), which gained prominence through Richard Brislin's (1986) work at the East-West Center in Hawaii for training professionals in intercultural communications and understanding. CIs are real-life problems and dilemmas that are to be reflected upon not so much for participants to find solutions but for participants to work backward from the critical situations to understand the various layers of causes that might have led to them. In the deconstruction of the incidents, participants reflect on how they could take advocacy steps to make a difference. In addition to exemplary practices, participants also contribute CIs to the Inquiry Learning Forum (ILF), a web-based repository funded by the National Science Foundation, where they can upload video footage for everyone in the forum to reflect upon and deconstruct.

The online pathways of practice discussed in this section demonstrate that the facilities of the online medium expand its educational role beyond the technical innovation that it clearly is.

Conclusion

At one time, the main goal of online distance education was creating access. As I show in this chapter, the principle of access is still important in that it provides teachers and their colleagues, wherever they are in the world, access to each other's support and expertise. However, the use of reflective pedagogy to frame online instruction also demonstrates that the special properties of the medium enhance its capacity to promote deep understanding and insight in the pursuit of knowledge. The asynchronicity and connectivity of the online medium allow for sustained interactions and thoughtfully considered reflections independent of time and location. These properties support the efforts of teacher educators to guide prospective and practicing teachers to become co-constructers of a teaching knowledge base grounded in experience and practice, to collaborate with colleagues near and far, and to undertake critical interrogation about teaching in the larger societal context. Thus, the medium not only provides a home base for all the stakeholders in teacher education, it also enables the teacher and learners to be literally at home, so that their teaching lives and professional development are dynamically integrated to the benefit of both.

R Questions for Further Discussion

1. Besides those mentioned in this chapter, what qualities have you noticed in the online medium that makes it conducive to engaging your course participants in reflecting upon their teaching?

2. What asynchronous and synchronous activities have you put together so that reflections on teaching take place regularly in your online language teacher education classes?

3. In this chapter, we described how our teaching is informed by Garrison et al.'s (2000) practical inquiry model for online instruction as well as Van Manen's (1977) foundational model and Korthagen's (1999) reflective frameworks. Other possible models include Schön's framing and reframing in reflection framework (1983); Zeichner and Liston's (1996) dimensions of reflection; Jay and Johnson's (2002) dimensions of reflection; and Hatton and Smith's (1995) levels of reflection. If you have used these models, share with your colleagues how they have or have not been useful. Share also other reflective frameworks not mentioned here that could be of benefit to language teacher educators.

References

Akyol, Z., & Garrison, D. R. (2011). Assessing metacognition in an online community of inquiry. *Internet and Higher Education, 14,* 183–190.

An, H., Shin, S., & Lim, K. (2009). The effects of different instructor facilitation approaches on students' interactions during asynchronous online discussions *Computers & Education, 53*(3), 749–760.

Anderson, T., Rourke, L., Garrison, D. R., & Archer, W. (2001). Assessing teaching presence in a computer conferencing context. *Journal of Asynchronous Learning Networks, 5*(2), 1–17.

Athanases, S. Z., & Martin, K. J. (2006). Learning to advocate for educational equity in a teacher credential program. *Teaching and Teacher Education, 22,* 627–646.

Bailey, K. M., Curtis, A., & Nunan, D. (1998). Undeniable insights: The collaborative use of three professional development practices. *TESOL Quarterly, 32*(3), 546–556.

Baran, E., Correia, A. P., & Thompson, A. (2011). Transforming online teaching practice: Critical analysis of the literature on the roles and competencies of online teachers. *Distance Education, 32*(3), 421–439.

Belenky, M. F., Clinchy, B. M., Goldberger, N. R., & Tarule, J. M. (1986). *Women's ways of knowing: The development of self, voice, and mind.* New York, NY: Basic Books.

Brislin, R. (1986). A culture general assimilator: Preparation for various types of sojourns. *International Journal of Intercultural Relations, 10*(2), 215–234.

Clark, D. B., & Sampson, V. (2008). Assessing dialogic argumentation in online environments to relate structure, grounds, and conceptual quality. *Journal of Research in Science Teaching, 45*(3), 293–321.

Eylon, B. S. (2000). Designing powerful learning environments and practical theories: The knowledge integration environment. *International Journal of Science Education, 22*(8), 885–890.

Ferris, S. P. (2002). Writing electronically: The effects of computers on traditional writing. *Journal of Electronic Publishing, 8*(1). Retrieved from http://quod.lib.umich.edu/j /jep/3336451.0008.104?rgn=main;view=fulltext

Freeman, D. (2002). The hidden side of the work: Teacher knowledge and learning to teach. *Language Teaching, 35,* 1–13.

Freeman, D., & Johnson, K. E. (1998). Reconceptualizing the knowledge-base of language teacher education. *TESOL Quarterly, 32*(3), 397–417.

Garrison, D. R. (2003). Cognitive presence for effective asynchronous online learning: The role of reflective inquiry, self-direction and metacognition. In J. Bourne & J. C. Moore (Eds.), *Elements of quality online education: Practice and direction* in Volume 4 in the Sloan C Series (pp. 29–38). Needham, MA: The Sloan Consortium.

Garrison, D. R. (2007). Online community of inquiry review: Social, cognitive, and teaching presence issues. *Journal of Asynchronous Learning Networks, 11*(1), 61–72.

Garrison, D. R., Anderson, T., & Archer, W. (2000). Critical inquiry in a text-based environment: Computer conferencing in higher education. *The Internet and Higher Education, 2*(2–3), 87–105.

Garrison, D. R., Anderson, T., & Archer, W. (2001). Critical thinking and computer conferencing: A model and tool to assess cognitive presence. *American Journal of Distance Education, 15*(1), 7–23.

Hatton, N., & Smith, D. (1995). Reflection in teacher education: Towards definition and implementation. *Teaching and Teacher Education, 11*(1), 33–49.

Havelock, E. E. (1986). *The muse learns to write: Reflections on orality and literacy from antiquity to the present.* New Haven, CT: Yale University Press.

Henri, F. (1991). Distance learning and computer-mediated communication: Interactive, quasi-interactive or monologue? In C. O'Malley (Ed.), *Computer supported collaborative learning* (pp. 145–161). Berlin: Springer-Verlag.

Jacobs, J. E., & Paris, S. G. (1987). Children's metacognition about reading: Issues in definition, measurement, and instruction. *Educational Psychologist, 22*(3–4), 255–278.

Jay, J. K., & Johnson, K. L. (2002). Capturing complexity: A typology of reflective practice for teacher education. *Teaching and Teacher Education, 18*(1), 73–85.

Kanuka, H., Rourke, L., & Laflamme, E. (2007). The influence of instructional methods on the quality of online discussion. *British Journal of Educational Technology, 38*(2), 260–271.

Korthagen, F. A. (1999). Linking reflection and technical competence: The logbook as an instrument in teacher education. *European Journal of Teacher Education, 22*(2–3), 191–207.

Korthagen, F. A. J. (2001). *Linking practice and theory: The pedagogy of realistic teacher education.* Mahwah, N.J.: Lawrence Erlbaum Associates.

Korthagen, F., Loughran, J., & Russell, T. (2006). Developing fundamental principles for teacher education programs and practices. *Teaching and Teacher Education, 22*(8), 1020–1041.

Korthagen, F. A., & Kessels, J. P. A. M. (1999). Linking theory and practice. Changing the pedagogy of teacher education. *Educational Researcher, 28*(4), 4–17.

Kyriacou, C. (1994). Reflective teaching in a wider context. In A. Peck & D. Westgate (Eds.), *Language teaching in the mirror: Reflections on Practice* (pp. 3–8). London: Center for Information on Language Teaching and Research.

Ong, W. J. (1982). *Orality and literacy.* New York, NY: Routledge.

Pawan, F., & Honeyford, M. A. (2009). Academic literacy. In R. F. Flippo & D. C. Caverly (Eds.), *Handbook of college reading and study strategy research* (2nd ed.; pp. 26–46). New York, NY: Routledge.

Pawan, F., Paulus, T. M., Yalcin, S., & Chang, C. F. (2003). Online learning: Patterns of engagement and interaction among in-service teachers. *Language Learning & Technology, 7*(3), 119–140.

Pawan, F., & Thomalla, T. G. (2005). Making the invisible visible: A responsive evaluation study of ESL and Spanish language services for immigrants in a small rural county in Indiana. *TESOL Quarterly, 39*(4), 683–705.

Pawan, F., Yalcin, S. T., & Kuo, X. J. (2008). Teaching interventions student factors in online collaboration. In B. Barber & F. Zhang (Eds.), *Handbook of research on computer-enhanced language acquisition and learning* (pp. 406–423). Hershey, PA: IGI Global.

Peck, A., & Westgate, D. (Eds.). (1994). *Language teaching in the mirror: Reflections on practice.* London, England: Center for Information on Language Teaching and Research.

Pennycook, A. (1999). Introduction: Critical approaches to TESOL. *TESOL Quarterly, 33*(3), 329–348.

Richards, J. C., & Lockhart, C. (1994). *Reflective teaching in second language classrooms.* Cambridge, UK: Cambridge University Press.

Schön, D. A. (1983). *The reflective practitioner.* New York, NY: Basic Books.

Van Manen, M. (1977). Linking ways of knowing with ways of being practical. *Curriculum Inquiry, 6,* 205–228.

Zeichner, K. M., & Liston, D. P. (1987). Teaching student teachers to reflect. *Harvard Educational Review, 57*(1), 23–48.

Zeichner, K., & Liston, D. (1996). *Reflective teaching.* Introduction. Mahwah, NJ: Lawrence Erlbaum Associates.

CHAPTER 3

Applying Universal Design for Learning to Inclusive Teacher Education in an Intensive Online Workshop

Faridah Pawan

Inclusive education is about how we develop and design our schools, classrooms, programs and activities so that all students learn and participate together
—*Community Living Ontario, 2014, p. 2*

Introduction

Educational professionals constantly seek new and better ways to make learning engaging and worthy of students' intellectual participation in the co-construction of knowledge. At the core of this pursuit is finding ways to help students access appropriate resources and make use of them. This is not an easy job as students in any one classroom may come from diverse language, cultural, and socioeconomic backgrounds; have multiple abilities; and be at different starting points.

Consequently, inclusiveness is a key issue in creating learning environments that avoid marginalizing students, especially those who are not in the mainstream. The field of special education has dealt with this issue extensively, producing a body of research that is enlightening to related fields, including English as a foreign language/English as a second language (ESL/EFL) pedagogy. ESL/EFL and special education overlap in their mission to accommodate the linguistic and cultural diversity of learners and serve those who have special language and communication needs. According to 2009 U.S. Department of Education statistics, 21% of school-age children speak a language other than English at home, and by 2025, 25% of all students in American schools will be both learning English as a second language and using it to learn other subjects (U.S. Department of Education, National Center for Education Statistics, 2012). Despite a longstanding history of misidentification of English learners (ELs) as candidates for special education services (Sullivan, 2011), typically these two areas have been treated separately and handled by very differently trained education specialists. However, the emergence of "inclusive education" as a framework has enabled educators to cross boundaries and work together to find ways to help all students experience "all facets of education in ways that address their unique needs" (Community Living Ontario, 2014, para 1). Inclusive education is an approach to education in which all learners are welcomed into all class settings. In fully inclusive learning environments, there is no distinction between "general" or "special" education classes.

Gargiulo and Metcalf (2013) stipulate that for education to be considered inclusive, educators must work to remove the barriers that may impede or exclude some students' meaningful participation. To ensure equal access for all learners, educators must rethink traditional paradigms of course design and delivery. The first step in this transformation is for instructors to recognize whom they are marginalizing with their existing instructional design. Then, they must consider how they can change their design to provide accessibility and scaffolding for all learners. The degree that a technology is able to be accessed by a wide variety of users represents its accessibility. Universal design for learning (UDL), a rights-based pedagogical framework grounded in learning sciences and neurocognition, is a useful tool to help teachers embrace the diversity of their 21st-century classes. In this chapter, after discussing UDL and how the online medium supports it, I describe a one-week intensive online UDL workshop for preservice ESL and world language teachers as they participated in a field experience that involved observations and practice teaching in public school classrooms.

Universal Design for Learning

Universal design for learning (UDL) is a framework for "for understanding how to create curricula that meet the needs of all learners" (CAST, 2011), which originated in 1984 at the Center for Applied Technology (CAST). This organization was founded to identify and explore technologies that could improve the educational experiences of students with disabilities (CAST, n.d., para. 2). However, since that time, CAST has broadened its mission to provide technologically accessible methods and materials that improve education for all learners.

Traditionally, the onus of accessibility has been on individual users or specialized support service providers. This meant that students were tasked with seeking out solutions for their own special needs or seeking help from support services when these were available. Universal design for learning, however, disperses the responsibility for inclusivity across all stakeholders, not only students, but teachers, support personnel, and curriculum designers as well. Also, rather than focusing on remediation that would somehow fix learners, educators using a UDL approach work to remove or reduce barriers to create new learning spaces and opportunities. Three primary principles undergird the UDL framework: multiple means of representation (MMR), multiple means of action and expression (MMA), and multiple means of engagement (MME). These guiding principles, often referred to as the 3Ms (Gargiulo & Metcalf, 2013), are the foundation for the framework's guidelines and curriculum checkpoints (Table 3.1). They are grounded in research on three prominent brain networks: recognition networks, strategic networks, and affective networks (CAST, 2011; Meyer, Rose, & Gordon, 2013). Rose and Strangman (2007) highlight the parallels between the three pillars of UDL and "what Vygotsky identified as

R TABLE 3.1. CAST'S PRINCIPLES AND CHECKPOINTS FOR UDL

Multiple Means of Representation (MMR)	Multiple Means of Action and Expression (MMA)	Multiple Means of Engagement (MME)
Guideline 1: Provide options for perception ← Checkpoint 1.1: Offer ways of customizing the display of information ← Checkpoint 1.2: Offer alternatives for auditory information ← Checkpoint 1.3: Offer alternatives for visual information	Guideline 4: Provide options for physical action ← Checkpoint 4.1: Vary the methods for response and navigation ← Checkpoint 4.2: Optimize access to tools and assistive technologies	Guideline 7: Provide options for recruiting interest ← Checkpoint 7.1: Optimize individual choice and autonomy ← Checkpoint 7.2: Optimize relevance, value, and authenticity ← Checkpoint 7.3: Minimize threats and distractions
Guideline 2: Provide options for language, mathematical expressions, and symbols ← Checkpoint 2.1: Clarify vocabulary and symbols ← Checkpoint 2.2: Clarify syntax and structure ← Checkpoint 2.3: Support decoding of text, mathematical notation, and symbols ← Checkpoint 2.4: Promote understanding across languages ← Checkpoint 2.5: Illustrate through multiple media	Guideline 5: Provide options for expression and communication ← Checkpoint 5.1: Use multiple media for communication ← Checkpoint 5.2: Use multiple tools for construction and composition ← Checkpoint 5.3: Build fluencies with graduated levels of support for practice and performance	Guideline 8: Provide options for sustaining effort and persistence ← Checkpoint 8.1: Heighten salience of goals and objectives ← Checkpoint 8.2: Vary demands and resources to optimize challenge ← Checkpoint 8.3: Foster collaboration and community ← Checkpoint 8.4: Increase mastery-oriented feedback

(Continued on page 32)

TABLE 3.1. *Continued*

Multiple Means of Representation (MMR)	Multiple Means of Action and Expression (MMA)	Multiple Means of Engagement (MME)
Guideline 3: Provide options for comprehension ← Checkpoint 3.1: Activate or supply background knowledge ← Checkpoint 3.2: Highlight patterns, critical features, big ideas, and relationships ← Checkpoint 3.3: Guide information processing, visualization, and manipulation ← Checkpoint 3.4: Maximize transfer and generalization	Guideline 6: Provide options for executive functions ← Checkpoint 6.1: Guide appropriate goal setting ← Checkpoint 6.2: Support planning and strategy development ← Checkpoint 6.3: Facilitate managing information and resources ← Checkpoint 6.4: Enhance capacity for monitoring progress	Guideline 9: Provide options for self-regulation ← Checkpoint 9.1: Promote expectations and beliefs that optimize motivation ← Checkpoint 9.2: Facilitate personal coping skills and strategies ← Checkpoint 9.3: Develop self-assessment and reflection

Adapted from *Universal Design for Learning Guidelines Version 2.0,* by CAST, 2011, Wakefeld, MA: Author. Copyright 2011 by CAST. Used with permission.

three essential learning constituents: recognition of information to be learned, application of strategies to process that information, and engagement with the learning task" (p. 382).

To implement the first guiding principle, multiple means of representation, educators need to provide students a wide range of choices for content representation and perception. Key features of MMR include offering customizable options for display and information input through multiple media formats, as well as providing support for "decoding of text and symbols" and "understanding across languages" while highlighting patterns, relationships, "critical features [and] big ideas" (CAST, 2011). The second principle, multiple means of action and expression, encourages the development of "strategic, goal-directed learners" (CAST, 2011). Guidelines for MMA include providing "options for expression and communication" through varied methods of navigation that optimize access to multimedia assistive technology tools and "building fluencies with graduated levels of support for practice and performance" (CAST, 2011). The final guiding principle, multiple means of engagement, involves providing options for recruiting interest, sustaining effort and persistence, and promoting self-regulation (CAST, 2011). MME guidelines call for reducing threats and distractions in learning environments and optimizing learner choice and autonomy by providing a range of requirements and materials to challenge diverse learners (CAST, 2011). As shown in Table 3.1, the checkpoints listed under each of the nine UDL guidelines lead sequentially to a target goal for the governing principle. The ultimate goals of the framework are for students to attain comprehension through the use of internal and external resources; strategically monitor and plan by means of their executive and meta-cognitive functions; and take ownership of their learning to sustain expertise.

UDL provides educators a framework for designing instruction and making information readily accessible. Perhaps most important, it also provides pedagogy grounded in a philosophy of inclusivity that combines flexibility with ways for adaptations to be systematic. This concept of flexibility within order has led Jimenez, Graf, and Rose (2007) and Lopes-Murphy (2012) to recommend incorporating UDL into the training of teachers who will work with English language learners. Indeed, training is needed for all educators to be able to move beyond discussions about inclusivity into realizing it in actual learning environments.

UDL and Online Instruction

The online medium provides an effective platform to model teaching and learning using UDL principles in large part because materials can be provided and represented in multiple ways—the multiple means of representation principle (MMR). Online delivery of materials includes options that are impossible in traditional face-to-face learning situations, which have fewer options for input and interaction. Online courses typically use a learning management system (LMS), which is a software application used to design and deliver e-learning. These systems, such as Blackboard, Oncourse, and Canvas, offer flexibility not found in print. As Edyburn (2011) points out, "whereas printed text is fixed (size, color, spacing), the physical appearance of digital text can be altered by the user, converted from text to audio, and translated from one language to another" (pp. 40–41). Customizable displays, such as zoom, color inversion, motion reduction, and high contrast in programs like Zoom Text and Kaltura, also provide multiple ways of representation. Among LMS features that can be used to enhance material, Canvas allows instructors to add subtitles and captions to create multiple layers of input and provide voice commands and spoken text to supplement written texts to ensure full comprehension. Text to speech (TTS) applications are also available that can translate text into audio formats. For example Kurzweil 1000 is scanning and reading software that can convert text into speech, which can then be modified in terms of speed, pitch, and emphasis. It also has features that facilitate web-based search and retrieval of information and online publications.

In preparing materials, instructors can incorporate online software packages with accessibility checkers (e.g., Adobe Acrobat) that alert them to potential barriers within their materials and provide feedback on both how and why to address the situation. The software can also provide instructors with scaffolding feedback, such as alerts to errors and tips that support making purposeful decisions about levels of inclusivity in course materials.

In line with UDL's principle of the multiple means of expression (MME), instructors can include other online applications to help students express themselves. For example, Co:Writer 4000, a type-and-speak writing assistant, helps with word prediction as the writer types or speaks sentences. Inspiration, on the other hand, uses graphic organizers to help writers map and concretize their ideas. Dragon NaturallySpeaking helps students control word processors using voice commands. Instructors will find many such assistive technologies that can help them use the online medium to apply UDL principles to promote inclusive education. The online medium combined with digital media is also optimal for supporting student engagement and action (MMA; see Chapter 6, "Dialectical Learning: Synchronous Meetings in an Online Language Research Class").

The asynchronous and synchronous nature of online learning aligns naturally with UDL in that it allows for multiple means and multiple time frames for engagement. Instructors can make provisions for students to engage with the content, classmates, and instructors in various ways: orally, visually through customizable display, or bimodally with both oral and visual information. In addition, the aspect of anytime and anywhere assures that learning time can be stretched, and students can participate at times best suited to their personal workflow preferences and, therefore, when they are at their cognitive peak. Synchronous tools such chat and instant messaging included in most online learning platforms provide options for instructors to profit from real-time dialectical interchanges (see Chapter 5, "Active Learning through Just-in-Time Teaching in a Hybrid and Flipped Doctoral Seminar"). Online synchronous communications have the advantages of multimodal engagement and the immediacy of face-to-face communications while buffering some of the distractions of physical presence.

The combination of the online medium with UDL principles is especially effective for supporting preservice teachers when they are taking initial steps into the field.

Guidelines for an Intensive Online Unit Incorporating UDL Principles

The unit described here was part of the field experience connected to an online ESL methods course for approximately 10 to 15 preservice teachers who were observing and coteaching in local public schools. I teach the methods course but monitor and draw from students' experiences in the field as part of the class, which has its own field supervisor. For the methods class, the students electronically sent in reflections on their field experiences to the weekly class online discussion forum. Inclusive education came up as one of the topics of reflections as students noticed the complexity involved in lesson and curriculum design given the diversity of students in the classrooms they were observing. To be immediately responsive as the methods course instructor, I put together an intensive one-week online workshop on UDL as a framework to guide students while they were observing and participating in classroom teaching. The online medium proved to be timely and relevant in this workshop not only for its capacity to provide resources to students while they were in the field but also, as mentioned above, for its quality as a ready-made platform to explore the potential of UDL.

The first consideration in designing the intensive online workshop was to develop guidelines to sustain student motivation and investment. Terminology for the guidelines was borrowed from Bonk and Khoo (2014, pp. 32–39) to conceptualize learning theories used, namely the principles of goal setting autonomy and curiosity, disequilibrium and variety, responsive feedback-and-encouragement cycle, and community and relevance. Table 3.2 also shows how the guidelines for the workshop were aligned with three of CAST's (2011) UDL implementation guidelines: explore, prepare, and integrate. The two remaining UDL guidelines, scale and optimize, were left for later discussions of what students could do as practicing teachers in their future places of employment to sustain their UDL expertise and promote a system-wide approach to the framework's integration and implementation.

TABLE 3.2. INTENSIVE ONLINE WORKSHOP GUIDELINES AND IMPLEMENTATION OF UDL IN PRESERVICE TEACHER UNIT

Intensive Online Workshop Guidelines	Implementation of UDL in Unit
a. **Goal setting autonomy and curiosity principle:** Instructors guide students to intentionally set individual and group goals for each day, the outcome of which they do not know but will get a chance to determine through their own creativity. Students report outcomes to each other at the end of each day.	Undertake needs assessment and explore the goals for change.
b. **Disequilibrium and variety principle:** Instructors develop problem-based settings so students could explore, inquire, interpret, reflect upon, judge, and construct new understandings.	Prepare and align resources.
c. **Responsive feedback-and-encouragement cycle principle:** Instructors of the course are present and engage daily with students, providing feedback and support to individuals and to groups. Peer scaffolding is equally essential in this principle. Teacher presence prevails over teaching presence (see Chapter 1, "Teaching Presence in Online Teaching") in this situation.	Integrate through instruction, facilitation, scaffolds, and evaluation.
d. **Community and relevance principle:** Instructors prioritize development of an online community by setting up multiple channels for private and public and collaboration. A sense of authenticity emerges through students' sustained interactions with fellow practitioners and instructors as well as a sense of identification and relevance with issues they share.	Integrate through community of practice.
e. To be implemented in teachers' own schools	Scale.
f. To be implemented in teachers' own schools	Optimize.

Pathways of Practice: Lesson Redesigns

Along with two associate instructors, I led the face-to-face planning for the 5-day intensive workshop, during which we determined observation sites, discussed UDL principles, developed materials, and planned activities, including prepping the preservice teachers to undertake needs assessment and data collection during observations and reflections afterwards. At the beginning of each 24-hour "online" day of the unit, students declared their goals, and at the end of each day they shared how they had achieved those goals with their collaborators. The workshop culminated in each student redesigning an existing lesson used by the cooperating teacher he or she was observing, showcased on online tools such as Glogster, Nota, or Magnoto. The students created digital posters, which can be considered online canvases or virtual spaces where items and media can be designed, moved, and manipulated (Hodgson, 2010). The posters were then shared via Oncourse, one of Indiana University's learning management systems in conjunction with the conferencing software, Adobe Connect, which allows for multipoint connection so students can share and collaborate on documents and materials in real time.

In the first activity the preservice teachers were asked to focus on the types of scaffolding they observed to address the background and ability diversity present in their respective classrooms. A chart (Table 3.3; Pawan, 2008) was provided as a guide for the preservice teachers to direct their observations to the four teaching scaffolding areas (linguistic, conceptual, social and cultural) and organize and display their findings at the end of the first day.

In line with CAST's suggestions ("About Universal Design," n.d.), I also developed a student profile example that demonstrated the need for cultural scaffolding for students similar to the one described (Figure 3.1).

To serve students such as the one profiled in Figure 3.1 in accordance with UDL principles and in culturally responsive ways (see Table 3.3), I indicated that that following steps had to be undertaken in the pre-service teachers' lesson redesign:

- MMR: To create a foundation for determining reading content, activate students' background knowledge and/or use popular media. Add bibliotherapy (Cohen, 1992), or using books of students' personal choice, the content of which resonates with students' backgrounds. Plan multimodal presentation of information to provide additional information to aid comprehension and make linguistic support for structural components available.

- MMA: Create options for students to communicate and engage with first language (L1) and second language (L2) peers as well as with their teachers, including simple to complex problem solving strategies and assessment tools (e.g., rubrics) to enable students to monitor own progress and create their own pathways toward success.

- MME: Ensure students are given the autonomy to select ways to express themselves using strategies they know and in configurations they are comfortable with.

TABLE 3.3. SCAFFOLDING TYPES

Scaffolding Type			
Linguistic Simplifying and making the "English" language more accessible	**Conceptual** Providing supportive frameworks for meaning providing organizational charts, metaphors etc.	**Social-Cultural** Mediating and situating students' learning in a social context involving the engagement and support of others (expert and novice, peer and peer; social). Also using artifacts, tools and informational sources that are specifically culturally and historically situated within a domain familiar to learners (cultural)	
		Social	Cultural
← Free journaling ← Prewriting ← Oral presentation of materials ← Reading out loud ← Conversational mode in lesson delivery ← Written instructions ← Simplified language ← Slowed pacing ← Direct instruction of form and meaning ← Direct instruction of form ← Vocabulary teaching ← Reading instruction	← Modeling ← Show instead of explain ← Body language ← Think alouds ← Structured step & choices ← Preteaching difficult concepts ← Frequent practice test sessions ← Bookmarking relevant websites ← Explicit connections between in-class and out-of-class experiences (life experiences) ← Explicit/transparent expectations ← Sourcebooks ← Condensed material ← Computers ← Realistic/authentic artifacts ← Visuals ← Charts ← Checklists ← Posters ← Pictures ← Simulations ← Experiments ← Games	← Teacher one-to-one assistance and encouragement ← Pairing English language learners with native speakers ← Combination of individual and group work ← Peer-coaching on assignments ← Specific role assignment in small groups	← Students' prior knowledge ← Literature from students' culture ← Students' learning styles ← Level 1 peer work ← Spanish speaking teacher colleagues for translation and instruction

Note. Adapted from "Content-Area Teachers and Scaffolded Instruction for English Language Learners" by Faridah Pawan, 2008, *Teaching and Teacher Education, 24*(6), 1450–1462.

FIGURE 3.1. PROFILE EXAMPLE

Student 1

A newcomer who has been in the United States for about 3 months, the student is a non-native speaker of English. He placed in level 3 because he is able to read passages in English at the intermediate level. However, he is often unable to explain what he has read. It is unclear whether he does not understand what he reads or he has difficulty expressing himself verbally in English.

When asked to write down his ideas, the student is often reluctant but gets involved in putting down ideas that others contributed when he works in a group. However, he ends up working individually with the teacher because he often gets frustrated with his classmates, who cannot read as fast as he can. Nevertheless, in these one-to-one engagements with the teacher, he often withdraws into himself.

I then showcased a redesigned problem solving lesson to engage students in conversations on the topic of the Gordian Knot. I had designed the lesson (Pawan, 2000; see Figure 3.2) using WebQuest (Dodge, 1995), an online inquiry tool. Figure 3.2 below shows only the opening part to the lesson for high school students or students in intensive English college matriculation class who have intermediate and high proficiency in English. The problem-solving lesson engages students to converse and discuss as they seek for solutions before they find out that Alexander had found a shortcut to solving the problem by cutting the knot. I developed the guidelines that accompany this part of the lesson so that the preservice teachers can see how I used UDL in my planning to support students in this part of the lesson.

 ## FIGURE 3.2. REDESIGNED GORDIAN KNOT LESSON

The Gordian Knot

In the winter of 333 B.C.E., the Macedonian general Alexander and his army arrive in the Asian city of Gordium to take up winter quarters. While there, Alexander hears about the legend surrounding the town's famous knot, the "Gordian knot." A prophecy states that whoever is able to untie this strangely complicated knot will become king of Asia. The story intrigues Alexander, and he asks to be taken to the knot so that he can untie it. He studies it for several moments, but after fruitless attempts to find the rope-ends, he is stymied. "How can I unfasten the knot?" he asks himself (see van Oech, 1983, pp. 47–48; and Hyldreth, 2015).

How can you help Alexander? According to the legend, the knot is the only obstacle standing in the way of him becoming king of Asia. What are some of your suggestions?

(Continued on next page)

FIGURE 3.2, *Continued*: GORDIAN KNOT LESSON

Here are some sample suggestions from those who've attempted to solve this challenge:

Celtic Inspired Knots
from Vector.me
(by kattekrab)

a. Choose one cord in the knot and follow it to its end, painting the chord with a bright color as you go along to keep track of it.
b. Drop the knot in water until it loosens.
c. Shake the knot vigorously.

Can you guess what Alexander did? The ways he solved the Gordian knot puzzle is proof that the reason Alexander became great was not because he did things the conventional way!

WEBQUEST

Multiple Means of Representation		
Checkpoints	**Scaffolding/Performance Assistance**	**Tools Utilized**
↘ Activate or supply background knowledge (3.1) ↘ Clarify vocabulary and symbols; syntax and structure (2.1, 2.2) ↘ Offer ways of customizing the display of information (1.1)	→ Stories from home describing Alexander the Great → Picture of Gordian knot provided → Essential words highlighted and meanings provided in call-out boxes → Unit is in text and audio format	← Oral or written stories from home about heroes and/or about Alexander the Great ← *Indiana Jones and Last Crusade* movie (1989; e.g., Netflix) ← Bibliotherapy (books of choice) ← Translator (Google or target language speaker) ← Text to speech (e.g., Announcify, Orato) ← Readability Index check (e.g., Flesch-Kincaid; (Fresch, 1948) ← Bilingual Dictionary/ thesaurus; collocation dictionaries ← Student personal dictionary (students provide their own definitions of critical words)

(Continued on page 40)

FIGURE 3.2, *Continued*: **WEBQUEST**

Multiple Means of Action and Expression		
Checkpoints	**Scaffolding/Performance Assistance**	**Tools Utilized**
↘ Use of multiple media for communication (5.1) ↘ Build fluencies with graduated levels of support for practice and performance (5.3) ↘ Enhance capacity for monitoring progress (6.4)	→ Multimedia options to work with language 1 peers, language 1 and language 2 peers, and/or with teachers → Range for problem solving strategies from easy to difficult → Rubrics to help students assess progress	← Chat websites (e.g., Zoho chat, Scriblar) ← Collaborative tools (e.g., TitanPad) ← Class time to connect ← Virtual hangout space (e.g., Google Hangout) ← Graphic information organizers (e.g., Thinkport) ← Rubistar (rubrics developer)
Multiple Means of Engagement		
Checkpoints	**Scaffolding/Performance Assistance**	**Tools Utilized**
↘ Optimize individual choice and autonomy (7.1) ↘ Facilitate personal coping skills and strategies (9.2)	→ Choice of presenting work in language 1, language 1 and English, or English → Choice of presenting written or orally in language 1, language 1 and English, or English → Choice of sharing work multimodally (e.g., through pictures and music) one-to-one or in groups	← Share verbally in person or via Voice Thread ← Paper or Digital Posters (e.g., Glogster, Nota, Magnoto) ← Teachers or Peers as Scribes ← Storytelling tools (e.g., ScrapBlog or Storybird)

The guidelines for an effective online intensive workshop (Table 3.2) were kept in mind during the 5 days of the unit. Beginning with the needs assessment of students in the classes they were observing to help in setting goals and to assess their achievement, the preservice teachers assembled the resources they shared to undertake changes to their cooperating teachers' lesson plans. Using Adobe Connect, I and the associate instructors responded promptly to all questions and invitations to review the preservice teachers' lesson redesigns in progress and in this way successfully sustained engagement. Using the same conferencing software, peers and instructors came together at the end of each day as a community of practitioners to look over and respond to each other's work while exchanging ideas. The weeklong intensive unit concluded with the sharing of the preservice teachers' lesson redesigns with digital posters developed on their choice of electronic platforms.

Final Considerations

The crux of the UDL principles is being responsive to students' needs. However, simply redesigning lessons cannot meet all the needs of all students. Thus, for teachers to be continuously responsive, constant communication with students and vigilance are needed throughout the implementation of a lesson.

Also, it is important to note here that no particular technologies, including digital media, are necessary for applying UDL to lessons (Rose, Gravel, & Domings, 2011, p. 8). Nevertheless, as Rose and Meyer (2002) note, technology can assist in shaping, extending, and transforming UDL efforts in education:

> The qualities of digital media most germane to education are their *versatility* (the ability to present information in any one of several media); their *trans-formability* (the capacity for content to be transformed from one medium to another); their capacity for being *marked*; and their capacity to be *networked*. (para. 20)

Rose et al. (2011) also point out that although there many different ways to provide options to students in UDL, at the practical level, it is advisable to offer a limited number of options at one time. Many students need time to get used to having options and opportunities to practice their use in ways aligned with their comfort levels and access, especially where technology is concerned. This learning curve requires time and repeated practice.

It must be noted here that options are important not only for learners but also for teachers preparing to incorporate UDL principles assisted by technology and digital media. For example, in undertaking the digital poster presentations in the intensive online workshop described above, the *TESOL Technology Standards* (2011) guidelines were used in providing them with four levels of technology and access options (Table 3.4).

The low tech/low access option consists of a fully accessible static visual display of information on a single PowerPoint slide. The mid tech/mid access option is a fully accessible static visual display of information with a scripted audio track and a transcript of the audio track. The redundancy of this bimodal option allows for less focus on the visual layout of the materials while still demanding careful consideration of the purposes and functions of each item on the single presentation slide. With the high tech/high access option, students create a dynamic visual display of multiple slides with accompanying audio tracks and text transcripts. Finally, the super high tech/high access option requires that both creator and audience have reliable access to high-speed broadband connectivity. This option, a TeacherTube video with close-captioned audio track and accompanying text transcript, offers several redundant modalities for presentation of the same content.

TABLE 3.4. WORKSHOP LEVELS OF TECHNOLOGY OPTIONS BASED ON TESOL TECHNOLOGY STANDARDS

TESOL Technology Standards (2008)	Low Tech/ Low Access	Mid Tech/ Mid Access	High Tech/High Access	Super High Tech/High Access
Suggested presentation Options	Accessible PowerPoint slide in PDF, (single medium)	Accessible PowerPoint slide with narration and audio track transcript (bimodal)	Accessible audio-visual presentation with transcript that is multimedia bimodal	TeacherTube video with subtitles and transcript

Note. Technology standards from *TESOL Technology Standards: Description, Implementation, Integration*, 2011, Alexandria, VA: TESOL Publications.

Conclusion

In this chapter I have described a multifaceted one-week online unit on UDL principles of inclusivity for preservice language teachers participating in a field experience. As UDL is being widely implemented in K–16 teaching contexts, it is important to prepare preservice teachers for jobs in which they are expected to be skilled in differentiation and design as well as to have experience using digital tools. Because a full range of tools is readily available in online learning management systems such as Oncourse, this venue is well suited for helping teachers realize the potential of inclusive English language learning and teaching.

R Questions for Further Discussion

1. Johnson (2009) distinguished between scaffolding and assisted performance; Scaffolding helps with "what is already ripening" (p. 23), that is, a process already begun, while assisted performance helps anyone to get through a task, even from the beginning. However, in this chapter, the two are considered stages of a single process. In designing your own UDL-aligned lessons, which position would you take and why?

2. Incorporation of principles of universal design first asks educators to the learner's position. How does this compare with previous paradigms? What specific practices might you question?

3. UDL asks instructors to think of themselves not just as content or pedagogical experts, but as instructional designers. How does reconsidering yourself as an instructional designer shed a different light on your practice?

References

Bonk, C., & Khoo, E. (2014). *Adding some TEC-VARIETY: 100+ activities for motivating and retaining learners online*. Bloomington, IN: Open World Books.

CAST. (2011). Universal design for learning (UDL) guidelines version 2.0. Wakefield: MA: Author. Retrieved from http://www.udlcenter.org/aboutudl/udlguidelines/downloads

CAST. (n.d.). About universal design for learning. Retrieved from http://www.cast.org /our-work/about-udl.html#.VdoYmPlVhBc

Cohen, L. J. (1992). Bibliotherapy. *Journal of Nurse-Midwifery, 37*(2), 91–94.

Community Living Ontario (2014). Our definition of inclusive education. Retrieved from http://www.communitylivingontario.ca/our-definition-inclusive-education

Dodge, B. (1995). WebQuests: A technique for Internet-based learning. *Distance Educator, 1*(2), 10–13.

Edyburn, D. L. (2011). Harnessing the potential of technology to support the academic success of diverse students. *New Directions for Higher Education, 154,* 37–44.

Flesch, R. (1948). A new readability yardstick. *Journal of Applied Psychology 32,* 221–233.

Gargiulo, R. M., & Metcalf, D. (2013). *Teaching in today's inclusive classrooms: A universal design for learning approach.* Belmont, CA: Wadsworth Cengage Learning.

Hanson-Smith, E., Healey, D., Hubbard, P., Iannou-Georgiou, S., Kessler, G., & Ware, P. (2011). *TESOL Technology Standards: Description, Implementation, Integration.* Alexandria, VA: TESOL Publications.

Hodgson, K. (2010). Digital posters: Composing with an online canvas. Chapel Hill, NC: Learn NC. Retrieved from http://www.learnnc.org/lp/pages/6542

Hyldreth, D. (2015). The Gordian Knot: Greek Oral History. Retrieved from http://www .damonart.com/story-gordionknot.html

Jimenez, T. C., Graf, V. L., & Rose, E. (2007). Gaining access to general education: The promise of universal design for learning. *Issues in Teacher Education, 16*(2), 41–54.

Johnson, K. (2009). *Second language teacher education: A sociocultural perspective.* New York, NY: Routledge.

Lopes-Murphy, S. (2012). Universal design for learning: Preparing secondary education teachers in training to increase academic accessibilty of high school English learners. *The Clearing House: A Journal of Educational, Strategies, Issues and Ideas, 85*(6), 226–230. Retrieved from http://dx.doi.org/10.1080/00098655.2012.693549

Meyer, A., Rose, D. H., & Gordon, D. (2013). *Universal design for learning: Theory and practice.* Wakefield, MA: National Center for Universal Design for Learning.

Pawan, F. (2000). Creative problem solving: A WebQuest for advance ESL students at the college level. Retrieved from http://www.usca.edu/education/courses/aete731/ss02 /Trainer/Creative%20Problem%20Solving.htm

Pawan, F. (2008). Content-area teachers and scaffolded instruction for English language learners. *Teaching and Teacher Education, 24*(6), 1450–1462.

Rose, D. & Meyer, A. (2002). Teaching every student in the digital age. Alexandria, VA: ASCD. Retrieved from http://www.cast.org/teachingeverystudent/ideas/tes/

Rose, D. H., & Strangman, N. (2007). Universal design for learning: meeting the challenge of individual learning differences through a neurocognitive perspective. *Universal Access Information Society, 5,* 381–391.

Rose, D. H., Gravel, J. W., & Domings, Y. M. (2011). UDL Unplugged: The role of technology in UDL. Manuscript submitted for publication. Retrieved from http://www.udlcenter.org/resource_library/articles/udlunplugged

Sullivan, A. L. (2011). Disproportionality in special education identification and placement of English language learners. *Exceptional Children, 77*(3), 317–339.

TESOL. (2011). *TESOL Technology Standards: Description, Implementation, Integration.* Alexandria, VA: TESOL Publications.

U.S. Department of Education, National Center for Education Statistics. (2012). *Digest of Education Statistics, 2011.* NCES 2012-001. Retrieved from http://nces.ed.gov/fastfacts/display.asp?id=64

Von Oech, R. (1983). *A Whack on the Side of the Head* (Vol. 58). New York: Warner Books.

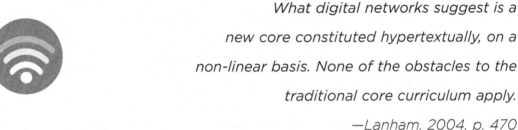

CHAPTER 4

Connectivism and Professional Development Across Large Groups

Crystal Howell and Ai-Chu Ding

What digital networks suggest is a
new core constituted hypertextually, on a
non-linear basis. None of the obstacles to the
traditional core curriculum apply.
—*Lanham, 2004, p. 470*

What knowledge is of most worth (Spencer, 1884)? For more than a century, education research has been shaped by this question. In the present digital age, this question takes on renewed importance. Lanham (2004) characterizes the expansion of curricula in the 21st century as freeing: geographic, temporal, and economic "obstacles to the traditional core curriculum" (p. 470) are toppled by the connectivity and accessibility promised by vast digital networks. Lanham's hypertextual utopia, however, is not a natural or inherent result of the simple proliferation of digital platforms across which large groups of people can connect. Researchers, practitioners, and students must approach such platforms cognizant of our digital agency. We are each the author of our own network, the hub around which other people and bodies of information are organized *by us*. As education gets "bigger"—exemplified by massive open online courses (MOOCs)—our networks become even more important, and our commitment to building them must become more deliberate.

In this chapter, we examine learning networks framed by the emerging theory of connectivism. Specifically, we will present the most current conceptualization of connectivism while situating it within preexisting learning theories. We will then define professional learning networks (PLNs) and explore how connectivism is realized by some of the various online platforms learners use to create their learning networks. We end our chapter with a practical discussion of our work on PLNs with preservice teachers in a teacher preparation program and with in-service teachers participating in a professional development (PD) series.

What Is Connectivism?

The concept of connectivism was first posited by Siemens (2004) just a decade ago. Siemens's conceptualization is largely based on the inability of existing learning theories to describe adequately how learners cope with exponentially increasing bodies of information. No longer can learners master a particular body of knowledge and expect their mastery to last a lifetime. Siemens cites Gonzalez (2004) when describing this modern phenomenon:

> One of the most persuasive factors is the shrinking half-life of knowledge. The "half-life of knowledge" is the time span from when knowledge is gained to when it becomes obsolete. Half of what is known today was not known 10 years ago. The amount of knowledge in the world has doubled in the past 10 years and is doubling every 18 months according to the American Society of Training and Documentation (ASTD). To combat the shrinking half-life of knowledge, organizations have been forced to develop new methods of deploying instruction. (para. 1)

Arbesman (2012) suggests that this reality sets new requirements for learners, perhaps the most important of which is that "we need to incorporate informational humility into our lives" (para. 10). Now in the digital age, information, a massive and constantly changing entity, is essentially unknowable.

Siemens's (2004) response to this changed reality is connectivism. Siemens's understanding of knowledge and learning relies upon Driscoll (2000), who aligns behaviorism, cognitivism, and constructivism with the epistemological traditions of objectivism, pragmatism, and interpretivism, respectively. In all three of these epistemological frameworks, Siemens asserts, "knowledge is an objective (or a state) that is attainable (if not already innate) through either reasoning or experience," and theorists and education researchers use the corresponding learning theories to explain how humans gather or create that knowledge (Background section, para. 3).

In connectivism, knowledge is conceptualized as the act of forming and engaging in networks with other learners, with organizational knowledge, and with stored information beyond the immediate recall of any given person. For example, while writing this chapter, we are utilizing connections between ourselves and our collaborators on this book (that is, other learners) as well as the academic community more broadly and the conventions of that community regarding research and writing (organizational knowledge). That community, and the research it encompasses, is contingent upon raw data (stored information), located in the hard drives and file cabinets of researchers around the world. Connectivism is epistemologically distinct, in that it asserts that all knowledge is not knowable or attainable. Contextualized within our digital age, connectivism embraces a rapidly changing, fluid conceptualization of knowledge. Learning, then, is not about attaining knowledge as its end. Siemens (2004) instead defines learning as

> a process that occurs within nebulous environments of shifting core elements— not entirely under the control of the individual. Learning (defined as actionable knowledge) can reside outside of ourselves (within an organization or a database), is focused on connecting specialized information sets, and the connections that enable us to learn more, are more important than our current state of knowing. (Connectivism section, para. 1)

Siemens characterizes knowledge itself (not just learning) as a verb, an action. According to Siemens, knowledge is connecting rightly across a network or networks. Other connectivist theorists, such as Downes (2006), echo this characterization. This is made clearer in Siemens's eight principles of connectivism (Figure 4.1).

Siemens sees connectivism as postbehaviorism, postcognitivism, and postconstructivism, identifying three primary limitations of these learning theories. First, he asserts that existing learning theories focus on the intrapersonal rather than interpersonal elements of learning. The core of knowledge and its acquisition are centered on the individual. Even constructivists, Siemens insists, "[promote] the principality of the individual" (2004, Limitations section, para. 1). Furthermore, he writes, these theories do little to explain or explore learning that exists outside of people, such as organizational learning or technologically situated learning. Finally, and most important, Siemens asserts that existing learning theories fail to address adequately the process of evaluation that occurs before learning

FIGURE 4.1. PRINCIPLES OF CONNECTIVISM

- Learning and knowledge rest in diversity of opinions.
- Learning is a process of connecting specialized nodes or information sources.
- Learning may reside in nonhuman appliances.
- Capacity to know more is more critical than what is currently known.
- Nurturing and maintaining connections is needed to facilitate continual learning.
- Ability to see connections between fields, ideas, and concepts is a core skill.
- Currency (accurate, up-to-date knowledge) is the intent of all connectivist learning activities.
- Decision making is itself a learning process. Choosing what to learn and the meaning of incoming information are seen through the lens of a shifting reality. While there is a right answer now, it may be wrong tomorrow due to alterations in the information climate affecting the decision.

From *Connectivism: A Learning Theory for the Digital Age* by George Siemens, 2004, Connectivism section, para. 3. Retrieved from http://itforum. coe.uga.edu/Paper105/Siemens.pdf actually happens, a "meta-skill that is applied before learning itself begins" (Limitations section, para. 2). In the digital world, this evaluative step is critical for "recogniz[ing] connections and patterns" (Limitations section, para. 2) and thereby plotting a course of learning through the modern information morass.

The Structure of Connectivism and the Role of the Online Teacher

As its name suggests, connectivism is about connecting and forming networks. As we mention above, within connectivism knowledge is characterized by action. Downes (2005) describes three kinds of knowledge: traditional qualitative knowledge, traditional quantitative knowledge, and what he calls "distributed knowledge" (Types of Knowledge section, para. 2). According to Downes, distributed knowledge that results from connections between entities is "connective knowledge" (Types of Knowledge section, para. 2). But connective knowledge is not merely all the facts that are known by the members of a given network. Connective knowledge resides not in a specific fact, but rather in the connection itself and in the interaction between actors (learners) at the point of connection. These points of interaction are called nodes. In nodes, learning communities form as more learners interact with one another and with information residing in digital devices. As more interconnected nodes form, the connections become a network. The goal of learners, thus, is not to master all the data encompassed by this network; rather, it is to be able to navigate the network swiftly, critically, and successfully to find relevant information. Figure 4.2 illustrates the central metaphor in understanding connectivism.

Nodes are learning communities or the points at which various learners intersect and interact. The entire network contains a vast amount of knowledge, some residing in

FIGURE 4.2. A VISUAL REPRESENTATION OF CONNECTIVISM

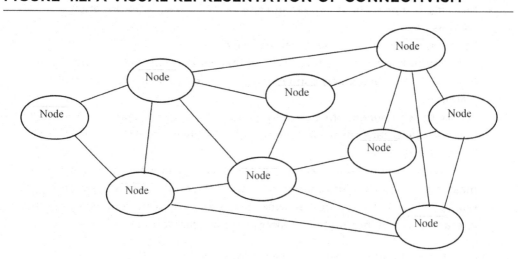

organizations or nonhuman appliances. Learning is made stronger by a greater number of linked nodes and facility in navigating the network.

What, then, is the role of the online teacher within connectivism? Brown (2006), Fischer (n.d.), Bonk (2007), and Siemens (2008) suggest a similar role, although each researcher names the role differently and highlights different qualities of the teacher and his or her actions. Brown (2006) describes an "atelier" model, a term borrowed from art studios and other contexts where creativity is vital and innovation important. In this model, the teacher acts as an expert, calling students' attention to and analyzing their innovations and successes. The students, however, are able to observe and comment on each other's work as well and so learn not only from the teacher but also from each other. Fischer (n.d.) calls the teacher a "network administrator" (para. 1), whose primary responsibility is assisting students in the formation and evaluation of a learning network. This learning network and students' proficiency working within it are contextualized by a particular set of objectives related to a class or content area. Bonk (2007) calls for a "concierge" model (para. 2) that emphasizes the teacher as proprietor of a domain who is at the service of students, guiding them toward resources that they might not explore on their own or even know existed. Siemens (2008) acknowledges these models and tweaks them a bit, calling the teacher a "curator" (p. 17). As such, the teacher compiles resources for students to explore (thereby exerting more control than Fischer's network administrator) and acts not only as an expert in the given field (as in Brown's atelier model) but also in navigating learning networks. In all four models, the teacher possesses expertise, but it is offered as a resource rather than a source of learning, and students possess markedly more agency than they do in classrooms that are more typical.

Connectivism Applied Online with Professional Learning Networks

At present, teachers and teacher educators are only beginning to apply the principles of connectivism to large-group online learning platforms. The experiences we describe in this chapter refer specifically to large groups of teachers and students harnessing the connective power of social-networking platforms (including Facebook and Twitter) not specifically designed as platforms to facilitate learning. In this section of the chapter, we examine professional learning networks (PLNs). In addition to defining PLNs, we discuss how they enact connectivist principles. Later in the chapter, we briefly shift our focus to MOOCs, a contrasting online platform designed specifically as a large group learning space.

The concept of PLNs is neither new nor unfamiliar in everyday life. On the contrary, most of us are already informally acquiring different domains of knowledge from our families, friends, and colleagues through social networking tools such as Facebook and Twitter. (Although we doubt that most Facebook or Twitter users would describe their activities this way!) Richardson and Mancabelli (2011) define a personal learning network as "a set of connections to people and resources both offline and online who enrich our learning" (p. 2). Personal learning networks in one sense are similar to social networks in that both stress connections and the social domain. However, professional learning networks are not merely social, as the change in name signifies. In PLNs, we do not connect with people just to know them—we connect with them to learn. The interactions within social networks are social exercises with learning perceived, if at all, as a by-product. In PLNs, on the other hand, we build connections with specific learning goals in mind. Although there are social elements in PLN interactions, the knowledge cultivated in a PLN primarily resides in the professional domain, and so PLN interactions are better categorized as intellectual rather than social exercises.

As understood via connectivism, knowledge is no longer a finite entity but rather a dynamic process, the lifelong activity of creating and critically engaging with networks of information. This is particularly evident for teachers, who are responsible for maintaining knowledge in a variety of domains: content knowledge, pedagogical knowledge, pedagogical content knowledge (Shulman, 1987), and technological pedagogical content knowledge (Koehler & Mishra, 2008). Professional learning networks, whether in preservice teacher education or in-service teacher PD, are crucial spaces for teacher learning, especially as they are enhanced by the affordances of the digital age. As connective technologies and knowledge expansion continue to reshape our curricula and students' ways of learning, we as teachers and teacher educators must respond. Teacher learning cannot be confined to schools of education. Instead, we must encourage teachers to expand their learning contexts and platforms to ensure lifelong professional learning.

PLNs are a powerful form of informal learning, allowing teachers to engage in personalized, accessible, reciprocal professional growth. PLNs allow teachers to personalize their professional learning experience by connecting to people and resources they find relevant to themselves and their situation. Unlike traditional (and often mandatory) PD, in which the content may or may not be relevant to participants, PLNs embody self-directed and self-motivated professional learning with which the learner may engage in ways related to his or her actual needs. Furthermore, in digital environments, PLNs allow this learning to occur anytime, anywhere. In traditional PD such as onsite workshops or seminars, teachers are bound by time and location. In PLNs, learning takes place in both synchronous and asynchronous forms via various social media and digital devices. A teacher can sit at a home computer to attend a webinar described in a fellow teacher's blog. The teacher can use a mobile phone to engage in a lively discussion on a Facebook PLN group while waiting for a bus. With the support of Internet connectivity and mobile technology, teachers can have nearly limitless flexibility and autonomy in terms of how their professional learning should take place. Finally, learning in PLNs can be reciprocal, social, and reflexive. In a PLN community (that is, a node), participants expect and benefit from reciprocal relationships. This reciprocity is critical for the sustainability and growth of PLNs. Each participant benefits from other participants' expertise and ideally engages reflexively with his or her own contributions. This reflexivity is "the instrument that translates teachers' experiences into dynamic knowledge" (Pawan, Chapter 2, "Tandem Certification Program for Indiana Teachers," p. 20).

Warlick (2009) divides PLN connections into three types: (1) personally maintained synchronous connections, (2) personally and socially maintained semisynchronous connections, and (3) dynamically maintained asynchronous connections.

Personally maintained synchronous connections. In synchronous PLN connections, learners engage in real-time interactions with other learners in the network to solve problems and accomplish goals together. The most obvious functional benefit of synchronous PLN connections is that learners' questions may be answered instantly. But one of the disadvantages is that learners are bound by time. Instant messaging and teleconferencing tools such as Skype, Adobe Connect, and Google Hangout are the most common platforms for synchronous connections, but live conferences and webinars are also platforms for synchronously connecting to experts and other practitioners.

Personally and socially maintained semisynchronous connections. Warlick (2009) characterizes semisynchronous connections as those that do not "have to happen in real time. Not only can the collaborators be geographically distant, but they can also participate in a discussion when it works best for their schedules, regardless of time zones or office hours" (p. 14). Semisynchronous connections occur in "conversations" composed of strings of asynchronous comments and posts within the network. Although learners may not receive instant response in semisynchronous connections, more participants may contribute, therefore enriching the node. Facebook, Google+, and Twitter are built around this type of connection.

For language educators, these platforms offer a variety of content-specific resources, such as #ELTChat, a weekly Twitter discussion group for teachers of English as a foreign language. Learners may participate synchronously in the weekly scheduled chat or asynchronously using the group-specific hashtag to find the conversation thread at a later time. Blogs, both personal and organizationally affiliated, are sites of semisynchronous connections. Practitioner blogs, such as Eva Buyuksimkesyan's (n.d.) Edublog Award–nominated A Journey in TEFL: My Adventure in Teaching, are vehicles for sharing teaching tools and resources while also creating a space for interaction (that is, a node).

Dynamically maintained asynchronous connections. Unlike the first two types of connections, which connect people to other people, the third type of PLN connection primarily connects us with "content sources that we have identified as valuable" (Warlick, 2009, p. 14). In synchronous and semisynchronous connections, communication is a two-way street, but in asynchronous connections, learners mostly participate in a network to receive information. This type of connection best illustrates Siemens's (2004) assertion that learning may be located within an organization or a nonhuman appliance. Siemens's own use of YouTube to store and distribute information about connectivist theory via video (e.g., Rheingold & Siemens, 2011) is an example of this type of connection. But the most central tools of asynchronous connections are actually rich site summary (RSS) aggregators and social bookmarking tools. Aggregators such as Feedly (http://feedly.com /index.html#welcome) and Netvibes (http://www.netvibes.com/en) allow learners to funnel multiple online sources into one site. Users subscribe to RSS feeds from individual sites and then organize and access them through a single aggregator dashboard, thus making nodes easier to access and new information less likely to slip through the cracks

Social bookmarking services such as Diigo (https://www.diigo.com/), Symbaloo (http://www.symbaloo.com/home/mix/13eOcK1fiV), and Pinterest (https://www.pinterest .com/) are also powerful tools for organizing and categorizing online sources but also give users the ability to publicly post their compiled resources. Sylvia Buller's language arts Symbaloo webmix (http://www.symbaloo.com/mix/languageartsinteractive) is an effective example of social bookmarking and demonstrates the increasingly complex network of nodes that learners can create.

Pathways to Practice: Introducing Preservice and In-Service Teachers to PLNs

In this section, both authors describe our work on teaching PLNs, Ding with preservice teachers completing a teacher education program and Howell with in-service teachers participating in a year-long PD series. In both examples, we are trans-classroom teachers (see Chapter 9, "The Trans-Classroom Teacher"), meaning that we move back and forth between teaching online and teaching face-to-face. As a note to our readers, in this section we describe work that we did separately; therefore, we refer to ourselves individually in the first person singular (I) or to ourselves and our colleagues at the time in the first person plural (we).

Ding Describes Online and Onsite PLN Work with Preservice Teachers

As a part of a semester-long, three hour course for preservice teachers focused on peda-gogically appropriate technology integration in language education as well as other content areas, my colleagues and I (Ding) developed an instructional website to engage class participants in learning about and creating a PLN (http://falloney83.wix.com/pln-for -educators). We overtly connected PLNs to professional growth and real-world educator empowerment via a variety of resources, including writings by practitioners and scholars. In our weekly face-to-face class, we asked students to build their PLNs through a variety of technology options, depending on their technological proficiency and preferences. After the class, they continued engaging with their PLNs online. Many students chose tools or platforms that they were already using socially. To engage students, we turned the entire learning process into a treasure hunt. From the beginning to the end of this learning module, we used a pirate adventure as a learning narrative, complete with pirate char-acters we created, a series of adventure-themed training events and tasks, and finally the ultimate treasure, a well-developed and engaging PLN. This adventure storyline, according to students' final evaluations, added a novel element to the course.

Providing appropriate scaffolding is essential to avoid unnecessary frustration and confusion for less tech-savvy learners. We injected scaffolding into the design of the website itself by including a curriculum map (presented as a treasure map; Figure 4.3), menu bar, and breadcrumbs. The treasure map made it easy for our students to evaluate

FIGURE 4.3. CURRICULUM MAP

their progress through the learning process, while the menu bar and breadcrumbs enabled learners to find target information and identify their location in the website with ease. In addition, we also created several job aids to support students' technology use. For example, if students opted to use Facebook to create their PLN, on the task page we provided a comic strip-style job aid (Figure 4.4; http://media.wix.com/ugd/33b7f2_63e6b227 e370a8167ba33043378a69b9.pdf) to help students focus on finding useful resources and learning communities rather than struggling to use the platform.

Simply having hands-on activities was not enough, however. For preservice teachers to transform their experience into dynamic knowledge, their reflections on their experiences and attitudes toward using technology must be critical and sustained (Tondeur, van Braak, Sang, Voogt, Fisser, & Ottenbreit-Leftwich, 2012). Therefore, in our PLN instruction, my colleagues and I engaged learners in individual and group reflection throughout the entire learning process. Some of this reflection occurred online before we worked with students in class. For example, before the class meeting, we asked students to watch an introductory video about PLNs and answer a series of questions. This activity

FIGURE 4.4. SAMPLE FACEBOOK JOB AID

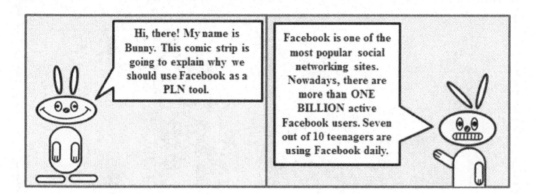

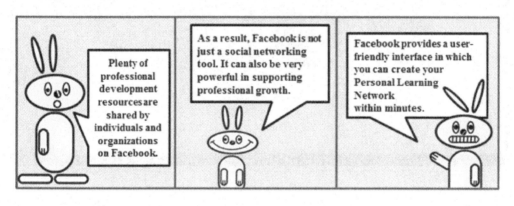

was part of the course's third and final unit, designed to synthesize students' growing technology skills with their pedagogical practices. We also asked students to reflect on their experience building a PLN, focusing on the effectiveness of their chosen platforms, how they had interacted with participants at their nodes, what had been most useful, and how their PLNs might enhance their professional learning, making it more effective and efficient. Then in our face-to-face class, we asked students to reflect on useful resources they had gathered from their PLN communities, strategies for building a PLN, and the potential risks and challenges of continued engagement.

Howell Describes PLN Online and Onsite
Professional Development with In-Service Teachers

After successfully integrating social networking in our National Writing Project Invitational Summer Institute, hosted by Coalfield Writers, a satellite site of the Marshall University Writing Project, my colleague April Estep and I (Howell) designed a year-long professional development series for in-service K–12 teachers committed to writing across the curriculum in their various content areas and inspired by the idea of building and maintaining a PLN. Our participants were all working professionals, scattered across three large, rural school districts in West Virginia. We designed the four-unit series to be completed over the course of an entire school year, with two units per semester. The first and fourth units included one face-to-face meeting in each unit, but the second and third units were completed entirely online. As many of our participants were social networking novices, our objectives were straightforward. We wanted learners to be able to (1) define, compare, and contrast social networks and professional learning networks; (2) understand the purposes and effects of participating in a PLN, and (3) successfully plan and implement classroom activities that incorporate educational networking and reflect on the effectiveness of these activities. Like Ding and her colleagues, we built our PD series on motivation, scaffolding, hands-on authentic experience, and reflection, but these components were realized differently within our context.

For our learners, motivation was much more related to technological dispositions and fear of another shallow PD than interest in or commitment to our PD series. Unlike Ding's students, who were completing a required course in their teacher education program, our in-service teachers were voluntarily completing the series and were eligible to do so only if they were also National Writing Project teacher consultants. Participants who completed the entire series received a small stipend. While their signing up for a PD series with a technology-related topic indicated their willingness to engage with technology and online platforms, our participants, like many in-service teachers, expressed anxiety about their skills. We sought to attenuate this anxiety and allow participants to tap into their existing tech skills more easily by engaging them in a physical and face-to-face networking exercise at the beginning of the first unit. We asked participants to stand in a circle and, using a brightly colored skein of yarn, we created a real, tangible network. As many had collaborated in previous National Writing Project events before, the teachers all had colleagues within the circle whom they knew shared some of their professional passions, and as they talked, they discovered previously unknown other connections. We concluded this activity with a discussion of the complexity of self-selected PLNs versus the narrowness of school-based professional learning communities (in which many of our participants were required to participate). Our in-service teachers' motivation, then, was rooted in two of Siemens's (2004) principles of connectivism: "learning and knowledge rests in diversity of opinions," and "nurturing and maintaining connections is needed to facilitate continual learning" (Connectivism section, para. 3). By affirming these principles in our opening unit, we were able to keep teachers' motivation high.

Also unlike Ding's students, many of our in-service teachers were not already active users of social media platforms such as Facebook, Twitter, and Instagram. Moreover, as working professionals, our participants were more acutely aware of their districts' specific acceptable use policies regarding which online platforms could be used at school, how they could be used (e.g., only for professional-to-professional PLN purposes or with students to create PLNs connected to a particular course or content area). Therefore, our scaffolding was threefold: we worked to support the in-service teachers' technology skills and their understanding of applicable district and state policies and precedents while also working to deepen their understanding of PLNs and improve their ability to navigate them successfully. Often this balance was achieved with patience and humor, as the sample starter activity in Figure 4.5 demonstrates. We also consciously selected resources from practitioner journals and practice-centered texts (specific examples included in Figure 4.5 are Hegna & Johnson, 2010; Huber, 2010; and Kist, 2010) to make new terms and concepts more accessible.

My colleague and I structured our four-unit series to be responsive to the calendars of our in-service teachers. Our first unit included a face-to-face meeting, as did our final unit. But the second and third units (during the busiest part of the school year) required participants to interact online. In this way, the delivery and structure of the series itself mirrored the structure of the PLNs that our participants were creating and with which they were engaging. These units included both common structured activities and activities that focused on individual decision making, such as thoughtfully adding to and engaging with new nodes. For example, all our in-service teachers were required to set up a Twitter account and follow the weekly #edchat during these units. In creating this common experience for analysis in the whole group, we acted as Siemens's (2008) curator-teachers, using a bounded range of resources to prepare our participants for independent evaluation of and engagement with other networking platforms and learning communities. Participants interacted asynchronously on a password-protected blog we administered, thus creating another shadow context for later independent interactions while also creating a space for reflection and discussion.

While learning to use a blog and interact with others' blog posts was one of our superficial goals for participants, we primarily used the blog to foster a reflexive approach to PLN development. As Ding and her colleagues did, my colleague and I wanted reflexivity to be an integral, constant part of creating, maintaining, or growing a PLN. Our fourth and final unit included a face-to-face meeting where our culminating activity was an extended reflection in which we asked participants to create snapshots of themselves both before and after their year of engagement in a PLN. Each participant shared his or

Learning the Lingo
Choose the best definition for the following terms.

1. Social networking
   a. Trading business cards with other professionals in your field.
   b. The interaction among a group of people who share a common interest.
   c. Anything that happens on Facebook or MySpace.
   d. Trading gossip with your coworkers next to the copy machine.

Answer: b. Social networking refers to the interaction among a group of people who share a common interest. As the term denotes, however, these interactions are primarily social; they are not necessarily connected to a person's professional life.

2. Educational networking
   a. The use of social networking technologies to communicate with other professional educators.
   b. The use of social networking technologies to communicate with students.
   c. The use of social networking technologies for educational purposes.
   d. The same thing as social networking, but it requires Department of Education certification.

Answer: c. In the March/April 2010 issue of *Library Media Connections*, Jen Hegna and Doug Johnson help teachers distinguish between social networking and "educational networking." Educational networking includes not only connections between teachers and other education professionals but also connections between teachers and students in "collaborative online learning experiences" that are a vital part of a modern education (p. 98). These types of interactions, like any other unit/lesson component, are well-planned and have specific educational purposes.

3. Web 2.0
   a. A term that encompasses a variety of web tools and services that focus on connections between users rather than solo use of the web.
   b. The newest fad web tool. Your principal will be monitoring your time in the computer lab to make sure that you're using it in your classes.
   c. Web 2.0? You were unaware that there was a Web 1.0.
   d. The latest web browser from Microsoft. You're going to have to uninstall Internet Explorer and then download it from Microsoft.com; it's sure to be a real pain.

Answer: a. In the handy mini-glossary accompanying her article "Professional Learning 2.0," Catherine Huber (2010) defines Web 2.0 as "a new generation of web services and applications that offer the opportunity to collaborate, share, and create content through social networking tools" (p. 43). More specifically, Web 2.0 tools require more than "passively view[ing] information that others have created"; instead, "users . . . interact with other users or edit content" (p. 43).

(Continued on page 58)

FIGURE 4.5. *Continued*

    4. New literacies
       a. Also known as textspeak. For example, "rotfl! btw, gotta go. c u l8r!!"
       b. Working with multiple forms of representation including books, magazines, webpages, music, video, blogs, wikis, etc.
       c. Something the foreign language teacher covers. It has nothing to do with me.
       d. I don't want to know—I like old literacies. Moby Dick, anyone?

Answer: b. In *The Socially-Networked Classroom*, William Kist (2010) describes his own inquiry process to define what a new literacies classroom looks like. He identifies five characteristics these classrooms share: (1) daily work in multiple forms of representation, (2) explicit analysis and discussion of different communication systems, (3) "think alouds by the teacher" when working with multiple kinds of texts, (4) "individual and collaborative activities," and (5) places "of student engagement in which students report achieving a 'flow' state" (p. 8)—that is, a state of intense and fulfilling focused engagement on a single task (Csikszentmihalyi, 1997).

    5. Blog
       a. A portmanteau word formed from the combination of "web" and "log." It is rather like a public journal, usually authored by one person and focused on a theme or topic.
       b. That website on which you typed your PLC book-study responses.
       c. A weather phenomena, kind of like "smog" but worse.
       d. Hey! You have a blog! You started it at an in-service you attended last year . . . wonder what that password was . . . hmm . . .

Answer: a. "Blog" is the combination of the words "web" and "log." It's an online journal; usually a blog has a theme. Readers can also usually comment on a blog.

---

her snapshots, and the resulting whole-group discussion dug deeply into Siemens's (2004) final principle of connectivism: "Choosing what to learn and the meaning of incoming information is seen through the lens of a shifting reality. While there is a right answer now, it may be wrong tomorrow due to alterations in the information climate affecting the decision" (Connectivism section, para. 3). This principle lies at the heart of meaningful engagement with PLNs. Every day, PLNs change, providing new information and linking participants with new colleagues or resources. Every day our participants changed as well, enriched by their connections. Successful learners, according to Siemens, are ultimately successful evaluators and navigators of their professional learning networks.

MOOCs and Connectivism

In discussing PLNs as a large-group learning platform, we must also mention massive open online courses (MOOCs), which, from our perspective, do not always align with connectivist principles in the way our design does for the teachers we work with.

Working backward through the name, MOOCs are first and foremost courses. Since 2001, the Massachusetts Institute of Technology's (MIT) OpenCourseWare (OCW), a progenitor of the MOOC, has made available the content of more than 2,000 MIT courses. Anyone can use MIT's OCW and ostensibly learn all that a traditional student in the same course might learn. In his explanation of how MOOCs came to be developed, Siemens (Rheingold & Siemens, 2011) describes how MIT's OCW makes content available instead of the learning process. Framed within connectivism, these two aspects are qualitatively different, and mere information, as Siemens (2004) asserts, is not sufficient in the connected, digital world. Knowledge is an activity—it is the ability to find, organize, evaluate, and critically engage with a network comprising information in the form of other learners, organizations, or devices. PLNs facilitate knowledge-as-action.

Furthermore, MOOCs are massive: they are open to registered students at host institutions but also to anyone else with Internet access and an interest in the course. When Stanford University first started offering MOOCs in 2011, it began with only three courses, for which more than 160,000 people registered. Theoretically, there are a limitless number of learners who might participate in any given course and a limitless scale of the network produced by the course, making it impossible for any one person to master the entire network. However, as Leckart (2012) points out, few students complete MOOCs. Their massiveness interferes with the development of meaningful connection and direct scaffolding in learning. In some ways, this causes MOOCs to revert to the old pedagogical model of one-way transmission. Will MOOCs make higher education accessible for a broad swath of the world's population who cannot afford a traditional college degree? Perhaps, although issues of access and structural limitations (such as free content but pay-for-certification models) already prevent many low-income users from using MOOC coursework as a stepping stone to more or better employment. Will MOOCs completely leave behind connectivist principles—particularly "nurturing and maintaining connections" between learners and other learners, not just learners and organizational or digitally stored knowledge (Siemens, 2004, Connectivism section, para. 3)—as they proliferate? We do not know, but it seems to be trending in this direction.

Reflections and Conclusion

For teachers and teacher educators, connectivism's reimagining of knowledge as an interactive, evaluative activity is a vital conceptualization of 21st-century learning. But this changed understanding of knowledge requires action from us as teachers. We must continue to develop new and better strategies for managing, navigating, and evaluating the ever-burgeoning body of information available to us online. At present, forming and maintaining PLNs is our best strategy for doing so.

R Questions for Further Discussion

1. How is knowledge conceptualized within connectivism? Does this conceptualization adequately differentiate connectivism from earlier learning theories? Is connectivism a learning theory or a curricular or pedagogical activity?

2. Have you ever considered participating in a PLN or MOOC? Why or why not? If you have done so or are doing so now, does your experience reflect the principles of connectivism outlined by Siemens (2004)?

3. Describe the differences in how "digital natives" and "digital immigrants" create and critically engage with PLNs (Prensky, 2001, pp. 1–2). How do these differences affect teaching PLNs to preservice teachers versus teaching PLNs to in-service teachers?

References

Arbesman, S. (2012, November 5). Be forewarned: Your knowledge is decaying. Harvard Business Review Blog Network. Retrieved from http://blogs.hbr.org/2012/11/be -forewarned-your-knowledge-i/

Bonk, C. (2007). *USA Today* leads to tomorrow: Teachers as online concierges and can Facebook pioneer save face? Retrieved from http://travelinedman.blogspot .com/2007/ 10/usa-today-leads-to-tomorrow-teachers-as.html

Brown, J. S. (2006, March). *Learning in the digital age (21st century).* Paper presented at the 7th Annual Ohio Digital Commons for Education (ODCE) Conference, Columbus, Ohio.

Buyuksimkesyan, E. (n.d.). A journey in TEFL: My adventure in teaching. Retrieved from http://evasimkesyan.com/

Csikszentmihalyi, M. (1997). *Finding flow: The psychology of engagement with everyday life.* New York, NY: Basic Books.

Downes, S. (2005, December 22). An introduction to connective knowledge. Stephen's Web. Retrieved from http://www.downes.ca/cgi-bin/page.cgi?post=33034

Downes, S. (2006, October 16). Learning networks and connective knowledge. Instructional Technology Forum: Paper 92. Retrieved from http://it.coe.uga.edu /itforum/paper92/paper 92.html

Driscoll, M. (2000). *Psychology of learning for instruction.* Needham Heights, MA: Allyn & Bacon.

Fischer, C. (n.d.). Teacher as network administrator. Retrieved from http://www.even fromhere.org/?p=374

Gonzalez, C. (2004). The role of blended learning in the world of technology. Retrieved from http://www.unt.edu/benchmarks/archives/2004/september04/eis.htm

Hegna, J., & Johnson, D. (2010). Guidelines for educators using social and educational networking sites. *Library Media Connection, 28*(5), 50–51.

Huber, C. (2010). Professional learning 2.0. *Educational Leadership, 67*(8), 41–46.

Kist, W. (2010). *The socially-networked classroom*. Thousand Oaks, CA: Sage.

Koehler, M., & Mishra, P. (2008). Introducing TPCK. In AACTE Committee on Innovation and Technology (Ed.), *Handbook of technological pedagogical content knowledge (TPCK) for educators* (pp. 3–29). New York, NY: Routledge.

Lanham, R. (2004). The implications of electronic information for the sociology of knowledge. In C. Handa (Ed.), *Visual rhetoric in a digital world: A critical sourcebook* (pp. 455–473). Boston, MA: Bedford/St. Martin's.

Leckart, S. (2012, March 20). The Stanford education experiment could change higher learning forever. *Wired*. Retrieved from http://www.wired.com/2012/03/ff_aiclass/

Prensky, M. (2001). Digital natives, digital immigrants. *On the Horizon, 9*(5), 1–6.

Rheingold, H. (interviewer), & Siemens, G. (interviewee). (2011, May 5). George Siemens on massive open online courses (MOOCs). Retrieved from http://www.connectivistmoocs.org/what-is-a-connectivist-mooc/

Richardson, W., & Mancabelli, R. (2011). *Personal learning networks: Using the power of connections to transform education*. Bloomington, IN: Solution Tree Press.

Shulman, L. (1987). Knowledge and teaching: Foundations of the new reform. *Harvard Educational Review, 57*(1), 1–22.

Siemens, G. (2004, December 12). Connectivism: A learning theory for the digital age. Retrieved from http://www.ingedewaard.net/papers/Connectivism/2005_siemens _ALearning TheoryForTheDigitalAge.pdf

Siemens, G. (2008, January 27). *Learning and knowing in networks: Changing roles for educators and designers*. Paper presented at the ITFORUM. Retrieved from http://itforum. coe.uga.edu/Paper105/Siemens.pdf

Spencer, H. (1884). *What knowledge is of most worth?* New York, NY: John B. Alden. Retrieved from http://books.google.com/books?id=D_gcAAAAMAAJ&printsec =frontcover&source=gbs_ge_summary_r&cad=0#v=onepage&q&f=false

Tondeur, J., van Braak, J., Sang, G., Voogt, J., Fisser, P., & Ottenbreit-Leftwich, A. (2012). Preparing pre-service teachers to integrate technology in education: A synthesis of qualitative evidence. *Computers & Education, 59*(1), 134–144.

Warlick, D. (2009). Grow your personal learning network: New technologies can keep you connected and help you manage information overload. *Learning & Leading with Technology, 36*(6), 12–16.

CHAPTER 5

Active Learning Through Just-in-Time Teaching in a Hybrid and Flipped Doctoral Seminar

Faridah Pawan

Learning is not a spectator sport. Students do not

learn much by sitting in classes listening to teachers,

memorizing pre-packaged assignments, and

spitting out answers. They must talk about what they

are learning, write about it, relate it to

past experiences, apply it to their daily lives.

—*Chickering & Gamson, 1987, p. 3*

In today's radically mediatized educational climate, where knowledge is considered fluid and ever changing, what is highly valued is students' ability to be active agents in shaping and transforming their own knowledge so that it develops in step with the evolving world around them (Pawan & Honeyford, 2007). In this chapter I focus on the pedagogy of active learning and just-in-time teaching (JiTT) in a hybrid and flipped semester-long seminar for advanced language education doctoral students, well-versed in their subject area.

Active learning (Bonwell & Eison, 1991) is a pedagogical approach that views students as "constructed knowers," a term derived from Belenky, Clinchy, Goldberger, and Tarule's (1986) description of individuals who view all knowledge as constituting a combination of who the knowers are, what they have experienced, and existing knowledge available to them, as well as the context in and means by which they communicate what they know.

Upon the interrogation and integration of what is known with what is unknown, these individuals create and invent (Piaget, 1974) knowledge as a means of understanding. In active learning, students are actively engaged in the knowledge construction and acquisition process rather than passively receiving one-way lectures. Much of students' preparation for active learning takes place outside class so that they are well-prepared for taking part in class activities, which generally involve collaboration, cooperation, and problem solving.

Just-in-time teaching (JiTT; Marrs & Novak, 2004), which is instruction that scaffolds rather than prescribes what is to be learned, is essential in undertaking active learning in the classroom. Instead of focusing on knowledge transfer, instructors engage alongside students and interact with them in thinking, answering questions, exploring and co-constructing ideas based on students' input on materials they read, activities they engage in, or problems they encounter before and while in class. This process, termed a feedback loop (Novak, Patterson, Gavrin, & Christian, 1999) is, thus, the opposite of the conventional just-in-case teaching (JiCT), in which instructors frontload information in the hope that students will find it useful in undertaking future tasks or challenges. Because teachers cannot predict all content that may be useful or relevant to students' future needs, the JiCT approach is to some extent a gamble, unless the tasks are tailored to fit the provided information, creating a closed system that negates active learning. Salman Khan's (2012) Khan Academy is a good example of a program that effectively employs JiTT. The academy supports students, parents and teachers in learning through 4,500 free video lessons on math, science, economics, computer programming and history. In these online lessons which consist of conversational web podcasts, students are in control of seeking help and information wherever, whenever, and at whatever level they need as they undertake a task or work to understand concepts. The success of the approach is supported by academy students' high levels of motivation and engagement and their achievement of learning goals.

Active Learning and Just-in-Time Teaching in a Hybrid and Flipped Seminar

Just as active learning and JiTT are mutually supportive, the former, by motivating student engagement and the latter by sustaining it, so are hybrid and flipped course formats. A hybrid class features both online and face-to-face instruction, and a flipped class converts the conventional classroom with one-way teaching into a collaborative space where instructors and students work together to co-construct knowledge. JiTT supports the hybrid, flipped classroom in the form of both soft and hard scaffolding (Saye & Brush, 2002; see Chapter 7, "Scaffolding in Online Process-Writing Instruction"). Soft scaffolding refers to teachers' focused attention to each individual student's activities, constant ongoing assessment of his or her learning needs, and provision of timely support. Hard scaffolds, on the other hand, are supports that can be embedded in instructional materials ahead of time (e.g., guiding questions). When computer software is used, hard scaffolds can be adapted to students' individual ability levels and task difficulty.

A seminar format provides an ideal setting for a hybrid, flipped class featuring active learning and JiTT pedagogies. A seminar usually consists of a group of advanced students, often seeking graduate degrees, who explore a topic in-depth by coming together to share knowledge, insights, and perspectives. During class meetings, they actively engage in Socratic dialogues and debates whereby they interrogate and deconstruct ideas with each other and with the instructor. Multiple perspectives are not only respected, but also regarded as essential to deep and nuanced understanding. Students prepare for this high-level critical dialogue by reading extensively and formulating ideas in writing so they are ready to bring important resources to the learning community. By virtue of students' access to almost unlimited knowledge and materials and the value placed on student-led construction of knowledge, a hybrid, flipped class draws on and develops the essential features of a seminar. In particular, the multimodal nature of the class fosters an expanded view of knowledge while it challenges conventional notions of "text" in ways that disrupt the hierarchical and developmental (simple to complex) sequence of learning and pushes participants to assume a heterarchical (Schwartz & Ogilvy, 1979) view of learning. Heterarchical learning emphasizes perspective over objectivity, and participants demonstrate intellectual growth in their ability to entertain and appreciate multiple and changing perspectives on issues. For example, the hypertext (texts that have words electronically linked to information and images) and multimodal nature of web pages requires readers to read using texts that Bolter (1999, pp. 459–460) describes as having the following characteristics:

- **Fluid and multilinear in content**. Material in hypertext is changeable, unstable, and unpredictable depending on the decisions readers make in terms of the order of presentation of the material read and the links to the material that the readers activate and consider relevant. Literate readers of hypertext believe that individual choices and decisions will make a difference in the reading experience and in the meaning derived from the reading.

- **Open and shared authorship with readers**. The readers' role is elevated to the status of collaborator in the authorship of hypertexts. The readers' presentation-order decisions and link choices make readers not only active collaborators in the construction of meaning in hypertext material but also critics who are aware of content and design shortcomings.

- **Multiple points of view requiring reader adjudication**. Readers of webpages often encounter a plethora of viewpoints that are organized primarily for reader access and consideration. Readers have increased responsibility to decide individually how these viewpoints converge into an argument. The deciding point will depend largely on what other materials and in what order readers choose to read in conjunction with the viewpoints presented on the web pages.

Students and teacher taking a heterarchical stance is essential in a hybrid and flipped class, in which learning takes place in a polymorphous and technology-mediated context (Thorne & Payne, 2005). A heterarchical stance also adds to and reaffirms the viability of goals that have been set for advanced students, such as the ability to think critically, undertake inquiry, analyze, problem solve, synthesize, take a position, communicate conflicting and informed perspectives, and impose a "framework of relevance" in a collaborative setting (Bolter, 1999, p. 460).

In the hybrid and flipped context with scaffolded learning, the concept of mentorworking, a workplace term, takes on new meaning. Mentorworking, usually used to describe workplace mentoring by more experienced colleagues or superiors, can also be extended to teacher education. Because of a graduate seminar's collaborative nature, it supports mentoring among students and between students and instructor, as well as between students and other experts. The seminar is a workplace in the true sense of a setting designed for productivity, one that enables the "meeting of the minds" between emerging and established academics. Through the use of web-conferencing technology, for example, instructors of a hybrid class can invite experts in the field into the classroom discourse so both the experts and the members of the classroom community can lead participants on new mental trips and provide just-in-time support. The classroom thus becomes a learning nexus without borders in which students can find intellectual mentors whose role is to guide students in evaluating, constructing, and resituating knowledge. Additionally, being able to network directly with professionals in the field is a practical benefit of hybrid classes. Such facility allows students to place discussions within grounded and lived realities. Bonk's (2012) definition of "extreme learning" as the ability to learn anything from anyone at any time, may be one of the greatest benefits of a hybrid and flipped class.

Finally, a hybrid, flipped class intensifies students' preparation for active learning in face-to-face class discussions in that they can use online discussion forums to familiarize themselves with foundational information, exchange understanding of readings, and select ideas that they want to explore in greater depth with each other and with instructors in real-time discussions. This allows face-to-face class time to be focused on the most pertinent issues. A hybrid class also facilitates collaboration and cooperation, in that online discussions allow for time to read and review positions so that students can formulate meaningful contributions. Reserved and less verbal students can express themselves and connect with others in a socially buffered environment. If there are conflicts or communicative misunderstandings, the online medium provides multiple opportunities for students to explain themselves and perhaps alleviate tension, deconstruct problems, and save face before they meet in class. In this way, too, students and instructors can establish the social presence they want to project (Rourke, Anderson, Garrison, & Archer, 1999) before face-to-face meetings. Finally, collaboration and cooperation can take place before and after as well as during class, as students have flexible and convenient access to their seminar colleagues.

The Socioconstructivist Foundation for Active Learning and JiTT in a Hybrid Classroom

The views of learning I discussed above have in common an emphasis on students' control over their own learning with consistent support by teachers and mentors, a basic principle of socioconstructivist theory. This theory views teaching and learning as social and scaffolded processes that emphasize students taking control of their own learning. Throughout the socioconstructivist learning process, teachers and other mentors provide consistent support for students. In the field of teacher education, as Huffaker and Calvert (2003) stated, this agency requires "curriculum methods and materials designed to allow students to apply concepts being learned to real-world contexts, build local and global communities of practice, and allow opportunities for learning in and out of the classroom" (p. 326). Inspired by Vygotsky, whose views are often contrasted with the cognitive-based philosophy of Piaget, socioconstructivism takes learning beyond the development of the individual's cognitive capabilities to emphasize the importance of interaction and communication in the construction of knowledge. In other words, Piaget (1974) focuses on the four internal changes (sensory, preoperational and concrete and formal operations) in learners' minds as they interact with their environment, although Vygotsky (1978) stresses the importance of conversations and socialization as a means for learning. Both, however, regard learners as active constructors of knowledge. The chart below is Bonk and Cunningham's (1998) interpretation of the principles as they relate to students in the classroom.

Table 5.1 by Bonk and Cunningham (1998, pp. 33–34) specifies points of difference between socioconstructivist theory, proposed by Vygotsky, and cognitive constructivist theory, first formulated by Piaget.

TABLE 5.1. SOCIOCONSTRUCTIVIST AND COGNITIVE CONSTRUCTIVIST PRINCIPLES

Social Constructivist Teaching Practices and Principles	Cognitive Constructivist Teaching Practices and Principles
Mind: The mind is located in the social interaction setting and emerges from acculturation into an established community of practice.	**Mind:** The mind is in the head; hence, the learning focus is on active cognitive reorganization.
Authentic Problems: Learning environments should reflect real-world complexities. Allow students to explore specializations and solve real-world problems as they develop clearer interests and deeper knowledge and skills.	**Raw Materials:** Use raw or primary data sources, manipulatives, and interactive materials.

(Continued on page 68)

TABLE 5.1. *Continued*

Social Constructivist Teaching Practices and Principles	Cognitive Constructivist Teaching Practices and Principles
Team Choice and Common Interests: Build not just on individual student prior knowledge, but on common interests and experiences. Make group learning activities relevant, meaningful, and both process and product oriented. Give students and student teams choice in learning activities. Foster student and group autonomy, initiative, leadership, and active learning.	**Student Autonomy:** Ask students for personal theories and understandings before any instruction. Allow student thinking to drive lessons and alter instruction based on responses. Place thinking and learning responsibility in students' hands to foster ownership.
Social Dialogue and Elaboration: Use activities with multiple solutions, novelty, uncertainty, and personal interest to promote student–student and student–teacher dialogue, idea sharing, and articulation of views. Seek student elaboration on and justification of their responses with discussion, interactive questioning, and group presentations.	**Meaningfulness and Personal Motivation:** Make learning a personally relevant and meaningful endeavor. Relate learning to practical ideas and personal experiences. Adapt content based on student responses to capitalize on personal interests and motivation.
Group Processing and Reflection: Encourage team as well as individual reflection and group processing on experiences.	**Conceptual Organization/Cognitive Framing:** Organize information around concepts, problems, questions, themes, and interrelationships, while framing activities using thinking-related terminology (e.g., classify, summarize, predict).
Teacher Explanations, Support, and Demonstrations: Demonstrate problem steps and provide hints, prompts, and cues for successful problem completion. Provide explanations, elaborations, and clarifications where requested.	**Prior Knowledge and Misconceptions:** Adapt the cognitive demands of instructional tasks to students' cognitive schemes, while building on prior knowledge. Design lessons to address students' previous misconceptions, for instance, by posing contradictions to original hypotheses and then inviting responses.
Multiple Viewpoints: Foster explanations, examples, and multiple ways of understanding a problem or difficult material. Build in a broad community of audiences beyond the instructor.	**Questioning:** Promote student inquiry and conjecture with open-ended questions. Also, encourage student question-asking behavior and peer questioning.

(Continued on page 69)

TABLE 5.1. *Continued*

Social Constructivist Teaching Practices and Principles	Cognitive Constructivist Teaching Practices and Principles
Collaboration and Negotiation: Foster student collaboration and negotiation of meaning, consensus building, joint proposals, prosocial behaviors, conflict resolution, and general social interaction.	**Individual Exploration and Generating Connections:** Provide time for the selection of instructional materials and the discovery of information, ideas, and relationships. Also includes encouraging students to generate knowledge connections, metaphors, personal insights, and build their own learning products.
Learning Communities: Create a classroom ethos or atmosphere wherein there is joint responsibility for learning, students are experts and have learning ownership, meaning is negotiated, and participation structures are understood and ritualized. Technology and other resource explorations might be used to facilitate idea generation and knowledge building within this community of peers. Interdisciplinary problem-based learning and thematic instruction is incorporated wherever possible.	**Self-Regulated Learning:** Foster opportunity for reflection on skills used to manage and control one's learning. Help students understand and become self-aware of all aspects of their learning, from planning to learning performance evaluation. Given the focus on individual mental activity, the importance of cooperative learning or peer interaction is in the modeling of and support for new individual metacognitive skill.
Assessment: Focus of assessment is on team as well as individual participation in socially organized practices and interactions. Educational standards are socially negotiated. Embed assessment in authentic, real-world tasks and problems with challenges and options. Focus on collaboration, group processing, teamwork, and sharing of findings. Assessment is continual, less formal, subjective, collaborative, and cumulative.	**Assessment:** Focus of assessment is on individual cognitive development within predefined stages. Use of authentic portfolio and performance-based measures with higher order thinking skill evaluation criteria or scoring rubrics.

Note. From "Searching for Learner-Centered, Constructivist, and Sociocultural Components of Collaborative Educational Learning Tools" (pp. 33–34) by C. J. Bonk and D. J. Cunningham, in C. J. Bonk and K. S. King (Eds.), *Electronic Collaborators: Learner-Centered Technologies for Literacy, Apprenticeship, and Discourse*, 1998, Mahwah, NJ: Lawrence Erlbaum. Copyright 2008 by C. J. Bonk and D. J. Cunningham. Reprinted with permission.

One of the best-known principles of socioconstructivism is Vygotsky's zone of proximal development (ZPD), the hypothetical space between what one can do or know and what one could do or know with adequate scaffolding and collaboration with knowledgeable mentors and peers. A key assertion is that our mental worlds are mediated and shaped by our lived experiences in our learning communities where we engage in dialoguing; idea and viewpoint sharing; and negotiating with peers and experts in meaning making, consensus building, and assessment. Just-in-time scaffolding is central in socio-constructivism as teachers' role as "guides on the sides" takes precedence over their role as "sages on the stage." Expert-to-novice as well as peer-to-peer and novice-to-novice mutual support is also a significant component of the theory. In this regard, growth through feedback is significant in that the contributions of many help build new structures of understanding and break through the knowledge status quo.

As a conceptualization of learning in school, the Bonk and Cunningham chart does not show the role of authentic practical experience, although it is a fundamental principle of socioconstructivism. Especially at the professional level, theory is derived from practice as well as circumstances in the real world, which generate knowledge that continually evolves as it is tested against new understandings, information, and experiences. As Kolb (1984) has pointed out, through his emphasis on "here-and-now concrete experiences" (p. 21) in learning, practical experience has origins in the theories of earlier influential scholars such as Lewin, Dewey, and Piaget and experiences are the bases for developing, testing and refining abstract ideas.

Instructors in a hybrid and flipped classroom thus need to create environments where students can actively engage in learning through goal-directed actions, evaluate the outcomes of these actions, and use this information to take further actions. In such an environment, students come to regard their ideas not as end points in the learning process but as beginning and interim points. Of vital importance are opportunities to engage with others, both peers and more knowledgeable mentors who can motivate and support students in their efforts to learn. I showcase several of these activities in the discussion that follows.

Pathways of Practice: Active Learning and JiTT in a Hybrid and Flipped Doctoral Seminar

The doctoral seminar described here is one that I teach for teachers and teacher educators that focuses on research into the professional development of language teachers. The semester-long (16 weeks) seminar meets 3½ hours weekly and involves students in original research on programs and activities that support second and foreign language teacher learning and that sustain their expertise. Although the limit is usually 12 students, the seminar generally attracts twice the number, including students who are auditing the class while they write their dissertations. The class meets face-to-face once a week in a physical class that has audio and video studio capabilities, enabling students located away from campus to join through five large screens in the class. Following the principles of flipped classrooms, where class time is to be spent on hands-on activities and engagement, during the face-to-face sessions, students consult peers and myself on their research projects. In addition, guest experts are regularly brought in via the online medium, not to lecture but to answer questions. Before class, students are expected to discuss, in an online discussion forum, the information from readings with peer. After class, they are expected to be online again along with me as a participant, to debrief, deconstruct, and assess new learnings that occurred in the face-to-face as well as the online discussions (see Table 5.2 for specific activities). I see the class as a hybrid class in that it blends the capacities of the face-to-face and online mediums in ways that support, reinforces and extend learning.

For active learning and JiTT to be in place in such a classroom, collaboration, as a fundamental social process, has to be taught directly and immediately. Much has been said about the importance of collaboration in teaching and learning in all platforms, (e.g., Dove and Honigsfeld, 2010; Echevarria and Graves, 2007) but it is infrequently taught.

At the beginning of the course, the students and instructors spend considerable time discussing collaboration and specifically online collaboration. We refer to resources such

TABLE 5.2. SEMINAR ACTIVITIES

Topic	Online preparation and research	Face-to-face collaborative and cooperative activities	Assessment	JiTT Scaffolding
Scope of language teachers' professional development	One week before class meeting, in groups of 3–4, students read and discuss articles uploaded in the class online discussion forum. Students may discuss the thrust of the articles, other related articles, their own experiences, and unresolved issues.	Students decide on unresolved issues that emerged from online discussions to discuss in class with other members of the group, the instructor, and invited guests.	a. Online participation frequency is automatically documented and calculated on the computer. b. Students assess classmates' participation according to moderating and leadership abilities, quality of resources shared, and insights that combine readings and experiences.	a. Instructor models discussion leadership and moderation during first 2–3 weeks of class. b. Instructor maps discussion patterns of groups to demonstrate effectiveness. (See Appendix 5.1 for examples.)

(Continued on page 72)

TABLE 5.2. *Continued*

Topic	Online preparation and research	Face-to-face collaborative and cooperative activities	Assessment	JiTT Scaffolding
Language program evaluation	Research and discussion on the online forum of language programs' evaluation frameworks.	Students meet with stakeholders and language program coordinators to undertake needs assessment. Students plan and develop program evaluation.	a. Evaluation plan and implementation assessed by stakeholders in face-to-face meetings b. Group evaluation of collaborations.	Evaluation consultants from TESOL headquarters brought in via videoconferencing software to respond to questions about language program evaluation.
Situated learning and praxis (training and practice convergence and/or disjuncture)	Interviews via videoconferencing tools with English language teaching (ELT) professionals who have recently returned to their home countries from study abroad to practice or those who have been practicing in the field. Interviews are recorded and live-chat transcripts archived.	Students share recordings. Discussion centers on identification of "disjunctures" and development of ways to "localize" and "vernacularize" language teaching approaches.	"Member checking" by ELTs interviewed in which they validate disjuncture identification and provide feedback on implementation of suggested localized approaches.	Instructor and students share experiences of convergences and disjuncture between training and practice.

(Continued on page 73)

as those provided by Pedagogy in Action (2010) whose cooperative learning elements we modified accordingly to our context:

1. **Positive interdependence**. The success of individuals is linked to the success of the group; individuals succeed to the extent that the group succeeds. (For example, students become involved in projects that they would be unable to undertake alone.)

TABLE 5.2. *Continued*

Topic	Online preparation and research	Face-to-face collaborative and cooperative activities	Assessment	JiTT Scaffolding
Publishing language-education professional-development research	Roundtable discussions with journal editors via videoconferencing technology.	a. Writing retreat where all participants write together for periods of three hours. b. Instructor and Peer feedback on research paper vis-à-vis editors' comments on manuscripts volunteered by students.	Submission of research papers for publication consideration.	Instructor shares own work and answers questions about reviews and comments from journal reviewers and steps taken to resubmit for publication.

2. **Individual and group accountability**. (I expanded accountability to include that of the group as well.) The group is held accountable for achieving its goals. Each member is accountable for contributing his or her share of the work; students are assessed individually. (For example, instructors familiarizing students with how to self-assess and to use crowd-source grading, that is, using students themselves as fellow graders.)

3. **Promotive interaction**. (I eliminated "face-face" from this label to include online interactions.) Students are expected to actively help and support one another. Members share resources and support and encourage each other's efforts to learn. (For example, instructors assigning roles to group members that capitalize on their strengths and allow the students to contribute meaningfully.)

4. **Development of teamwork skills**. (I replaced "Interpersonal and Small Group Social Skills" with this new subheading.) Students are required to learn academic subject matter (task work) and also to learn the interpersonal and small group skills required to function as part of a group (teamwork). Teamwork skills should be taught just as purposefully and precisely as academic skills. (For example, students learn to make distinctions between collaboration—working together to achieve mutually agreed upon goals—and cooperation—working together to achieve individual goals.)

5. **Group processing**. "Students should learn to evaluate their group productivity. They need to describe what member actions are helpful and unhelpful, and to make decisions about what to contribute or change" (Barkley et al., 2005, p. 9

as cited in Pedagogy in Action, 2010). (For example, the instructor encourages students to consistently reflect upon their actions and their relationship to the macro picture held by the group.)

Introducing students to online collaboration applications is important to enable them to work together. It is also essential that students do not engage in one-way blogging that is, following posts on social media or online discussions forums without intentional participation (lurking).

Active learning in this seminar begins with explanatory instruction that sets the stage for class procedures; then moves to guided inquiry, an intensely collaborative phase; and then to learning by doing, that is, applying knowledge and exploring its uses (Rusbult, 2007). These elements are implemented in tandem with Marrs and Novak's (2004) just-in-time teaching principles in which there are (1) "content transfer" to online preclass preparation and use of class (face-to-face) time on cooperative problem solving; (2) structured opportunities for students to actively and collaboratively construct new knowledge from prior knowledge; and (3) prompt feedback and assessment. Table 5.2 is representative of the seminar's online and face-to-face activities.

In this seminar, there are no lectures or emphasis on knowledge transmission but instead there is mentored and purposeful engagement; exploration; reflective actions; participation alongside the instructor; and feedback from peers, instructors and specialists. Throughout this process there is engagement in such higher order thinking skills as analysis, synthesis, and evaluation of thoughts and ideas made available multimodally and hypertextually. In other words, the hybrid and flipped quality of the class enables the juxtaposition of active learning and just-in-time teaching.

As discussed in Chapter 9 ("The Trans-Classroom Teacher"), through our numerous experiences of observing students, we are reminded that learning can take place even without overt interaction and engagement (Duffy & Kirkley, 2004). There are many students who choose to demonstrate their intellectual involvement not through active engagement in class but through their writing and in private one-to-one conversations. This shows that room has to be created for these individuals, pedagogically and in practice. Nevertheless, the online medium, particularly the asynchronous facility combined with collaboration in a hybrid class, is a viable avenue for these students to express themselves without the pressure of spontaneity and without the glare of direct and singular attention.

Conclusion

Means, Toyama, Murphy, Bakia, and Jones (2010) concluded that "instruction conducted entirely online is as effective as classroom instruction but no better. Blends of online and face-to-face instruction, on average, had stronger learning outcomes than did face-to-face instruction alone" (p. 19). Given this report and the discussions above, the convergence of hybrid classrooms with active learning and just-in-time teaching pedagogies increases the rigor and relevance of language teacher education.

Questions for Further Discussion

1. In this chapter, I have made the claim that and demonstrated how a hybrid and flipped class is a suitable setting for active learning and just-in-time pedagogies. What challenges do you see in implementing these pedagogies in your setting? How might you adapt these practices to overcome these challenges?

2. Many researchers distinguish between collaboration and cooperation, the former being group members working and being assessed together and the latter involving members working together but being assessed for individual work toward achieving common goals. Referring to your particular situation, how might this distinction affect strategies used in providing online or hybrid professional development to language teachers?

3. Freire's (1970) concept of praxis is centered on the idea that theory and practice inform and are transformed by each other. In your experiences as a teacher and teacher educator, how has this concept been manifested in a hybrid or face-to-face class? How would you assess the success of its application in each setting?

References

Belenky, M. F., Clinchy, B. M., Goldberger, N. R., & Tarule, J. M. (1986). *Women's ways of knowing: The development of self, voice, and mind.* New York, NY: Basic Books.

Bolter, J. D. (1999). Information technologies of the future of the book. In D. A. Wagner, R. I. Venezky, & B. Street (Eds.), *Literacy: An international handbook* (pp. 457–461). Oxford, UK: Westview Press.

Bonk, C. J. (2012). Technology enhanced teaching: From tinkering to totally extreme learning. *Proceedings of the 1st International Conference on Open and Distance Learning,* Manila, the Philippines (pp. 1–33). Retrieved from http://www.extreme-learning.org/news.php

Bonk, C. J., & Cunningham, D. J. (1998). Searching for learner-centered, constructivist, and sociocultural components of collaborative educational learning tools. In C. J. Bonk & K. S. King (Eds.), *Electronic collaborators: Learner-centered technologies for literacy, apprenticeship, and discourse* (pp. 25–50). Mahwah, NJ: Lawrence Erlbaum.

Bonwell, C. C., & Eison, J. A. (1991). *Active Learning: Creating Excitement in the Classroom. 1991 ASHE-ERIC Higher Education Reports.* ERIC Clearinghouse on Higher Education, Washington, DC: George Washington University.

Chickering, A. W., & Gamson, Z. F. (1987). Seven principles for good practice. *AAHE Bulletin, 39*(7), 3–7.

Dove, M., & Honigsfeld, A. (2010). ESL coteaching and collaboration: Opportunities to develop teacher leadership and enhance student learning. *TESOL Journal, 1*(1), 3–22.

Duffy, T. M., & Kirkley, J. R. (Eds.). (2004). *Learner-centered theory and practice in distance education: Cases from higher education.* Mahwah, NJ: Lawrence Erlbaum Associates.

Echevarria, J., & Graves, A. W. (2007). *Sheltered content instruction: Teaching English language learners with diverse abilities*. Pearson Allyn and Bacon.

Freeman, D. (2009). The scope of second language teacher education. In A. Burns & J. C. Richards (Eds.), *The Cambridge guide to second language teacher education* (pp. 11–19). New York, NY: Cambridge University Press.

Friere, P. (1970). The adult literacy process as cultural action for freedom. *Harvard Educational Review, 40*(2), 205–225.

Huffaker, D. A., & Calvert, S. L. (2003). The new science of learning: Active learning, metacognition, and transfer of knowledge in e-learning applications. *Journal of Educational Computing Research, 29*(3), 325–334.

Johnson, K. E. (2006). The sociocultural turn and its challenges for second language teacher education. *TESOL Quarterly, 40*(1), 235–257.

Johnson, K. E., & Golombek, P. R. (2003). "Seeing" teacher learning. *TESOL Quarterly, 37*(4), 729–737.

Khan, S. (2012). "The One World Schoolhouse," After Words (interview), C-Span video.

Kolb, D. A. (1984). *Experiential learning: Experience as the source of learning and development* (Vol. 1). Englewood Cliffs, NJ: Prentice Hall.

Lantolf, J. P., & Thorne, S. L. (2006). *Sociocultural theory and the genesis of second language development*. Oxford: Oxford University Press.

Marrs, K. A., & Novak, G. (2004). Just-in-time teaching in biology: Creating an active learner classroom using the Internet. *Cell Biology Education, 3*(1), 49–61.

Means, B., Toyama, Y., Murphy, R., Bakia, M., & Jones, K. (2010). *Evaluation of evidence-based practices in online learning: A metaanalysis and review of online learning studies*. Washington, DC: U.S. Department of Education Office of Planning, Evaluation, and Policy Development.

Novak, G., Patterson, E., Gavrin, A., & Christian, W. (1999). *Just-in-time teaching: Blending active learning with web technology*. Upper Saddle River, NJ: Prentice Hall.

Pawan, F., & Honeyford, M. (2007). Academic literacy. In R. F. Flippo & D. C. Caverly (Eds.), *Handbook of college reading and study strategy research* (pp. 26–46). New York, NY: Routledge.

Pedagogy in Action. (2010). *What is cooperative learning?* Retrieved from http://serc.carleton.edu/sp/library/cooperative/whatis.html

Piaget, J. (1974). *To understand is to invent: The future of education*. New York, NY: Grossman Publishers.

Rourke, L., Anderson, T., Garrison, D. R., & Archer, W. (1999). Assessing social presence in asynchronous, text-based computer conferencing. *Journal of Distance Education, 14*(3), 51–70.

Rusbult, C. (2007). *Effective teaching methods*. Topsfield, MA: American Scientific Affiliation. Retrieved from http://www.asa3.0rg/ASA/education/teach/active.htm

Saye, J. W., & Brush, T. (2002). Scaffolding critical reasoning about history and social issues in multimedia-supported learning environments. *Educational Technology Research and Development, 50*(3), 77–96.

Schwartz, P., & Ogilvy, J. (1979). *The emergent paradigm: Changing patterns of thought and belief*. Menlo Park, CA: SRI International.

Thorne, S. L., & Payne, J. S. (2005). Evolutionary trajectories, Internet-mediated expression, and language education. *CALICO Journal, 22*(3), 371–397.

Vygotsky, L. S. (1978). *Mind in society*. Cambridge, MA: Harvard University Press.

Appendix 5.1

Instructor's mapping of groups' discussion patterns.

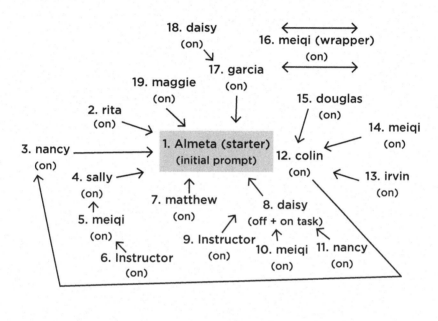

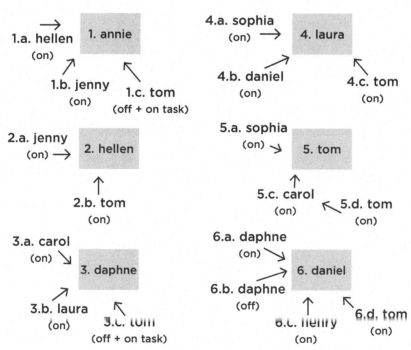

CHAPTER 6

Dialectical Learning: Synchronous Meetings in an Online Language Research Class

Amber N. Warren

To call inquiry a "stance" is to regard inquiry as a worldview, a critical habit of mind, a dynamic and fluid way of knowing and being in the world of educational practice that carries across professional careers and educational settings.

—Cochran-Smith and Lytle, 2011, p. 20

In an onsite class, spontaneous discussion and connection may take place in face-to-face settings. However, the proliferation of fully online programs suggests that there is a need to leverage available technology to provide students in online courses with more opportunities for interactive and practical course discussions, mirroring the experience of onsite education courses. So how do we bring this experience to the online classroom? One possibility is the addition of synchronous, or real-time, sessions, in which course participants meet to discuss or collaborate simultaneously. While much online communication happens asynchronously, or separated in time and space (e.g., forum discussions, blog comments), synchronous meetings occur when participants meet at the same time, often with voice and video capabilities. The multiple channels or modes available (e.g., text, audio, video) create an increased sense of immediacy in communication and feedback, which may expand participant engagement and thereby participant learning. This benefit of felt immediacy is one element of the theory of social presence applied to online communities (Rourke, Anderson, Garrison, Archer, 1999). Social presence, according to this theory, refers to the ability of a communicative space to support social and affective interactions, and it has been linked to levels of student participation, satisfaction, and engagement in online learning. Improvements in communication technology, such as multi-channel web-based conferencing platforms, make coming together in this space possible for participants physically situated in different parts of the globe. However, implementing productive synchronous sessions requires effective design and pedagogical support on the part of the instructor.

In this chapter I describe how one multichannel web-conferencing platform (Adobe Connect) was used to facilitate real-time collaborative discussion and enable peer and teacher support for students in a graduate online research course for English as a second language (ESL) teachers. I begin with a discussion of the dialectical theory of learning, according to which people learn through dialogue with one another. The theory provides the basis for the use of audio- and video-enhanced synchronous meetings as part of case study projects during an online pedagogy-of-writing-instruction course. Then I explore how technology enhances the affordances and opportunities for synchronous discussion. The meetings discussed under "Pathways of Practice" provide examples of actual discussion and learning in a spontaneous environment, illustrating a layer of interaction that helps reduce the distance in distance education and that allows for just-in-time responses to issues from both colleagues and instructor. Thus, this chapter is framed by two main tenets: that learning is a social process that takes place through interaction with others and that practitioners are uniquely positioned to increase our knowledge of how students learn within the everyday contexts of the schools in which they teach.

A Dialectical Theory of Learning

Dialectical learning is a social theoretical worldview grounded in Vygotsky's (1978) claim that learning and understanding are developed through social interaction using discussion and reasoning as the main means of knowledge development. Dialectical learning, therefore, encourages learners to examine issues open-mindedly with other people and from multiple angles. Much early educational research was premised on the belief that an individual's behavior was a sufficient lens into his or her cognition, (Brown, 1987; Sulzer-Azaroff, 1995) but critiques of this perspective emerged with Vygotsky's (1934/1962) seminal work, *Thought and Language*, in which he theorized that learning takes place through communication, most saliently with "more experienced others." Thus, cognition came to be understood as having both an individual and—significantly—a social basis. The idea that cognitive development occurs through mediated social interaction has since become a central tenet in a sociocultural view of education or what Stahl (2006) described as a social theory of learning. This perspective puts emphasis on meaning negotiation and dialogue. It is derived from Vygotsky's (1978) characterization of learning in childhood as "a complex dialectical process," in which development is not a straightforward process but is an uneven, complex process in which various functionalities develop in different orders, transforming and merging, and in which beliefs may be challenged by alternative perspectives and experience. Learning then involves practice and conversation, that is, a "knowledge-creation process" rather than a knowledge-transmission process

(Paulus & Phipps, 2008). This dialectic theory, in which discussion and reasoning are seen as means of development, has become a primary basis of educational theory today.

For example, traditionally delivered onsite ESL teacher preparation courses are often highly interactive and practical. Instructors frequently introduce material through the methods they hope students will use, and students are given numerous opportunities to practice the different methods, strategies, and techniques introduced in the course. This way of teaching is based on the assumption that people learn in dialogue with more experienced others. Additionally, research suggests that educators learn new methods of teaching through experiencing the methods for themselves (Trygvasson, 2009). Therefore, teacher education programs that include numerous opportunities to experience modeling followed by practice can influence participants' use of these methods in the future.

However, this kind of immediacy is not the only way to encourage dialectical learning in the teacher education classroom. In the online course described in this chapter, this social theory of learning is operationalized by using inquiry as a stance to guide preservice and in-service teachers in conducting case-study research to question and solve problems much as they will be expected to do day-to-day in their classrooms.

Practitioner Research, or Inquiry as a Stance

Sociocultural theory is based on the idea that learning is not just a matter of individual knowledge transmission but instead takes place within a social context that shapes the learning (e.g., Lantolf, 2000). Therefore, teachers, who have firsthand knowledge of that social context are well positioned to conduct research in the field. In practitioner research, also called practitioner-initiated research, preservice and in-service teachers engage in research involving learners in the settings in which they teach and can encourage them to explore the tensions that often exist between research and practice. Such practitioner-initiated research has been taken up in teacher education programs around the United States and has come to be known as "inquiry as a stance." According to Cochran-Smith and Lytle (2011), inquiry as a stance is "a theory of action grounded in the problems and contexts of practice," which places practitioner knowledge at the center of educational research (p. 20). In teacher education courses, students engage in practitioner-initiated research such as action research or case studies to pose questions, investigate issues, and solve problems encountered in teaching. Teacher educators in global settings have taken similar approaches. For instance, in Finland a master's teacher education program approached the goal of producing "pedagogically-thinking, reflective and inquiry-oriented teachers" (Toom et al., 2010, p. 339) by requiring teacher-students to behave "like researchers" by carrying out theoretically informed inquiry projects. The use of school-based research in teacher education programs has the potential not only to enhance "student teachers' professional learning through research" but also to add to knowledge about a research topic itself (Kershner & Hargreaves, 2012, p. 275).

Proponents of practitioner research frequently cite the benefits of embedding teachers' learning in their everyday work. Among these benefits are the increased likelihood that this learning will be meaningful (Lieberman, 1996) and potentially transformative (Price, 2001). As Cochran-Smith and Lytle (2011) pointed out

Inquiry and practice relate to each other in terms of productive and generative tensions, and they are understood to have a reciprocal, recursive, and symbiotic relationship. Thus it is not only possible, but also beneficial to take on simultaneously the role of both practitioner and researcher. (p. 19)

Kershner and Hargreaves (2012) have further observed that there is a "distinctive research position held by student teachers in crossing boundaries between school and university contexts" (p. 275). By encouraging students to actively engage in questioning and discussion at the cross-points of these contexts, practitioner-initiated, classroom-based research may encourage them to move away from a view of teaching as routinized activity toward a view of teaching as "intellectual and contemplative practice" (Lambe, 2011). Case studies, which offer a focused, in-depth look at one person or group of people within a specific context, can be conducted in a variety of ways. Thus, as a form of inquiry-guided practitioner research, they can be flexibly employed in a variety of settings and to a variety of ends and so offer almost limitless ways for students in teacher education courses to take ownership of their learning and professional growth.

Case Studies in Practitioner Inquiry

Case studies are used to answer questions that begin with how or why (Yin, 2003). Additionally, by exploring multiple characteristics of one particular case, case studies emphasize description and detail (Hammersley, 1995). Since the aim of case studies is to provide as full a picture as possible of a specific situation, they are quite applicable to single-learner or small-group inquiry. Their adaptable nature is a particular strength in a teacher education course in which students may be coming from a variety of settings. In the online writing pedagogy course described in this chapter, preservice and in-service teachers are invited to use either a descriptive or an intrinsic case study approach to focus on one particular learner over the span of the semester. A descriptive case study simply describes an intervention or phenomenon (Yin, 2003). Intrinsic case studies, as their name suggests, examine a particular case or phenomenon for its inherently interesting or unique properties. These are useful approaches when the researcher's goal is to deepen his or her understanding of the specific case (Stake, 1995). As Baxter and Jack (2008) put it, the case study "is not undertaken primarily because the case represents other cases or because it illustrates a particular trait or problem, but because in all its particularity and ordinariness, the case itself is of interest" (p. 548).

Boeher and Linsky (1990) characterize a case study as "a story; it presents the concrete narrative detail of actual, or at least realistic events, it has a plot, exposition, characters, and sometimes even dialogue" (p. 41). Although it may include descriptive quantitative data, a case study is a type of qualitative research designed to be exploratory in nature and is thus not meant to be replicable or generalizable in the way quantitative studies are (Creswell, 2011). The context, a natural setting such as a teacher's classroom, is of central importance. Therefore, when teachers take up case study research, they are asked to consider the uniqueness of the setting, as well as the learner's individual characteristics, in their research. As a form of practitioner inquiry, teachers may use case studies to improve their teaching and students' learning in a particular setting or for a particular event. In all cases, the purpose is not to generate a theory about learners in general but to gain transferable knowledge by better understanding a particular learner in a particular situation.

As they move between student and educator roles pursuing licensure or additional certification, both preservice and in-service teachers should take any opportunity to actively connect learning to practice, or they risk experiencing feelings of disconnect between their roles as teachers and learners (Calderhead & Robson, 1991). By adopting dialectical learning as an instructional framework, teacher educators can encourage their students to actively engage in questioning, negotiating meaning, and developing connections between classroom practice and theory. By using practitioner-initiated inquiry as a vehicle, dialectical learning encourages students to query, provoke, and develop their understanding to make these connections.

Affordances and Opportunities for Dialectical Learning in Synchronous Web-Conferences

Current language education theories support viewing knowledge as co-constructed and situated (see, for example, Brown, Collins, & Duguid, 1989; Firth & Wagner, 2007; Lantolf, 2000, and Chapter 4, "Connectivism and Professional Development Across Large Groups"). As online teaching continues to grow and technology continues to improve, the possibilities for including synchronous discussion in education increase. Therefore, taking advantage of the affordances of multichannel online classroom spaces may be a way to expand opportunities for dialectical learning, which is how traditional onsite ESL teacher preparation courses are often structured.

Although multichannel web-conferencing technology has been in use in universities for at least a decade, very little has been written on the use of this technology in fully online classes. Multichannel web-conferencing is Internet-based software that provides multiple means of communication for participants engaged in real-time (synchronous) communication and collaboration. The earliest research into the use of synchronous communication in distance education focused on text chatting, as video and audio capabilities were not yet advanced enough for synchronous communication and were frequently unreliable due to Internet speeds (Park & Bonk, 2007). However, with improvements in technology and increased Internet speeds and reliability, recent research in synchronous audio and video conferencing suggests enormous potential for its use in online teacher education.

Researchers have shown that there are many benefits to asynchronous distance education, including increased convenience and flexibility and additional time to reflect and craft responses (e.g., Garrison, 2003; see Chapter 2, "Reflective Pedagogy in Online Teaching"). However, wholly asynchronous, online courses have some drawbacks as well. For instance, students may feel isolated or that they are not able to interact fully with their instructor and peers (Vonderwell, 2003). Therefore, one benefit of synchronous meetings that include an audio or video component is that they offer increased immediacy, reducing psychological distance and improving students' motivation (Park & Bonk, 2007). Further, synchronous meetings provide opportunities for meaningful interactions and the introduction of multiple perspectives for solving problems (Park & Bonk, 2007). Taking advantage of the audio and video capabilities available in multichannel web-conferencing platforms may also allow for an experience closer to face-to-face communication by increasing students' feelings of social presence (Kear, Chetwynd, Williams, & Donelan, 2012) and rapport (Falloon, 2011). These qualities are all highly valued in dialectical learning.

To date, researchers have tended to focus more on technical affordances than on pedagogical aspects of synchronous multichannel communication. Studies largely show that faculty and students find it useful but often have concerns about reliability (Internet connectivity and speeds) and whether all participants have access to video or audio functions (e.g., Bower & Hellstén, 2010). Therefore, instructors seeking to incorporate synchronous meetings in their courses may need to be flexible with their expectations of participation, especially as students enrolled in online classes may reside anywhere in the world.

Some teacher educators have opted for synchronous web-conferencing to bring together students in far-flung regions of a country during their field experiences or internships. For instance, Steed and Vigrass (2011) used synchronous meetings with students in a teacher preparation program in Canada. The students were placed in internships at various schools in distant locations, making travel to campus for seminar meetings unfeasible. Although the problem had previously been addressed with the use of asynchronous discussion boards, in 2011 the instructors decided to use Adobe Connect in the seminar to allow students to see and hear one another. Although most of the first meeting was spent handling technical issues, these abated as students became more familiar with the technology. Additionally, at the start there was some confusion with turn-taking, but again, once students became accustomed to the software, conversation flowed naturally, and they were able to discard the formal turn-taking procedure implemented at the start of the course. Overall, students reported that they found the experience offered high-quality interaction and was satisfactory.

Student satisfaction and perception surveys suggest that, barring technology issues, students have found the experience of synchronous web-conferencing to be generally engaging and more satisfactory than wholly asynchronous courses (McGuire & Castle, 2010). Further, after students' initial introductions to the software, technology confusion is reduced (Ng, 2007) and overall they are able to communicate with one another effectively (Steed & Vigrass, 2011). However, technical issues may still have the strongest impact on students' self-reported feelings of autonomy. If students struggle with technical issues, this may negatively impact their feelings of social connection if they become preoccupied with technical procedures rather than their interactions with others (McBrien, Jones, & Cheng, 2009). These findings underscore the importance of teaching presence in the planning and designing phase. (See Anderson, Rourke, Garrison, & Archer 2001 and Chapter 4: "Connectivism and Professional Development Across Large Groups" of this volume for more on teaching presence.) While in-the-moment issues may still arise, pedagogical knowledge and careful direction as to when and how to use elements of the platform are key to successful implementation.

Findings suggest that one strength of synchronous meetings is that they can increase participant engagement through enhanced perception of social presence and teacher immediacy (e.g., Park & Bonk, 2007), and many researchers have noted that most students favorably evaluate the addition of such meetings to online classes (e.g., Bower & Hellstén, 2010; Steed & Vigrass, 2011). A major strength of using web-conferencing technology is the increase in dynamic interaction, as the communication is happening in real time. This dynamic interaction is central to a dialectical framework for learning, which encourages spontaneous discussion and dialogue.

While meaningful collaboration is perhaps difficult to attain in synchronous online settings, this does not diminish the potential for this medium to encourage dialectical learning, which relies on dialogue and exchange of multiple perspectives among participants. Moreover, asynchronous activities in online classes frequently rely heavily on learner-content interaction, in that typically students respond to readings through postings in a forum or blog. Even when forums are set up to encourage discussion, research has shown that engaging students in meaningful communication about a topic can be a challenge (Pawan, Paulus, Yalcin, & Chang, 2003). The inclusion of synchronous web-conferencing sessions in an appropriately learner-centered way encourages students to focus on each other's ideas through learner-learner interaction (Smyth, 2011). In a dialectical theory of learning, this type of interaction is central to increasing learners' critical thinking about a topic. Therefore, a dialectical theory of learning may be particularly suitable for framing activities in synchronous web-conferencing.

Considerations when Using Synchronous Meetings in Global Classrooms

The richness of the web-conferencing platform allows students to participate in experiences beyond the traditional lecture mode, including practice work, presentations, and group work. In that sense, it is much more like a student-centered face-to-face classroom. These platforms can even allow engagement and interaction in many configurations. However, in planning for effective synchronous meetings, course instructors must consider their own role, as well as the roles of the students and of the technology itself.

Students as stakeholders. Because students enrolled in the course may be situated anywhere in the world, the course frequently includes practicing teachers working outside the United States. Because of this, flexibility in scheduling online synchronous meetings is essential. The diversity of the student population and the educational settings to which they have access also necessitates that the scope of the case study assignment be broad so that all participants can complete assignments effectively and meaningfully. When the course contains larger numbers of students, or students from numerous time zones, providing more than one synchronous meeting time enables more students to participate with less inconvenience.

Instructors must also consider students' multiple perspectives. On the one hand, large numbers of international students come to the United States each year to study, and as the numbers of online courses increases, many of these students find themselves in hybrid or even fully online classes, even though they have traveled to the United States to study. On the other hand, as distance education programs become more popular, increasing numbers of students enroll in U.S.-based programs while retaining residence abroad. This diversity leads to different problems. For instance, Wang and Reeves (2007) found that Taiwanese students using web-conferencing in online classrooms reported having difficulty managing multiple channels of communication (e.g., text and audio) at the same time. And Kramsch and Thorne (2002) found that language students from different cultures adjusted to text-based mediums in various ways. When students moved to a synchronous text chat from email communication, all students adopted a less formal register, whereas the use of email resulted in varying levels of formality, depending on the background of the participants. These examples demonstrate the necessity of considering students' cultural backgrounds and prior experiences with online learning when planning synchronous meetings.

The instructor's role. Online instructors must take on the mantle of instructional designer when planning course interactions. As technology access increases, teachers need to pay attention to the affordances it offers to design more learner-centered activities, providing opportunities for learner-learner interactions. Instructors must be aware that their role should go beyond simply providing space for dialectical practice, which is not in itself sufficient to ensure that it will take place. According to Anderson et al. (2001), "a formal distance education course consists of much more than dialogue between and among teacher and students and includes course readings, web explorations, exercise and individual and collaborative projects" (p. 5). The notion of teaching presence encourages instructors to account for all these elements of their instruction from the beginning of the design phase and make sure that they all work together. Without attention to their part in the overall scheme, synchronous meetings may result only in aimless conversation. By giving purpose and structure to the meetings; by planning meetings at key moments in the semester; and by using them as a complement to activities, such as a case study; the instructor can create more opportunities for dialectical learning.

Technical support. In the course described in this chapter, the synchronous meetings were conducted using the Adobe Connect platform. However, any web-conferencing system will offer many of the same utilities. Essentially, web-conferencing platforms allow multiple participants to come together in one space and communicate in real time through audio, video, and text. They may also include a whiteboard space and the option to share screens and upload content, making the space into a virtual classroom. Additionally, the software enables the instructor to create small breakout groups within the class, allowing for pair or group discussions. This feature is advantageous in that it allows the instructor to increase student-driven discussion time. However, if investment in this platform is not feasible, free alternatives exist and may provide classrooms with many of the same capabilities (e.g., BigBlueButton, Google Hangouts).

Regardless of the platform selected, many students may initially be unfamiliar with its use. Introducing students to the platform early will enable them to familiarize themselves with the technology, rehearse its use at their own convenience before the class meeting time, and allow more of the synchronous time to be devoted to content-driven discussion. That being said, the start of the first meeting will likely be focused on technical issues. Anticipating this and planning the first synchronous lesson time accordingly will keep instructors from feeling rushed to cover planned material.

Developing a clear set of guidelines (or accessing guidelines developed by instructional consulting offices and providing them for the students) should be a part of the instructional supports offered early in the semester. A simplified technological guide can be designed to anticipate the early setup problems encountered when students are unfamiliar with the technology, ensuring that everyone can participate. While it may not be possible to predict technical problems that arise unexpectedly, recognizing that technology issues will likely arise can help instructors avoid some and handle others efficiently. Technical support, therefore, involves careful planning on the part of the instructor.

Pathways of Practice: Moving Dialectical Learning and Practical Inquiry Online

In writing-pedagogy courses, the instructor often works closely with learners to understand their particular needs and to help them develop effective plans for teaching based on theories and strategies introduced through course readings. When an English as a foreign language/English as a second language (EFL/ESL) course characterized by a highly diverse membership transitions to an online setting, the instructor must develop ways of providing support for all participants as they conduct a case study, often for the first time. Therefore, significant attention must be paid to providing learning experiences that are meaningful across a variety of instructional settings. Following is a description of the case study project that is the centerpiece of the master's level course in focus here: one of the offerings in a language teacher education online program that provides both certification and degree-seeking options.

Overview of the Case Study Project in a Writing Pedagogy Course

The master's level course discussed here is part of an English as a second language (ESL) certification program and lasts 15 weeks. The course is focused on pedagogy of writing instruction for ESL teachers and surveys themes and issues in the theory and practice of teaching writing to language learners. Topics of study include learner identity, evaluation and feedback, the roles of grammar and vocabulary in writing, and models of writing instruction (e.g., process writing and genre-based approaches). The major assignment in the course is a case study, which is broken into a series of steps, or smaller assignments, that are combined to create a completed case study at the end of the semester. In the first weeks of class, the participants are asked to find a student who will become the focus of their case study. Each subsequent course assignment builds on the last, scaffolding the teachers' progress toward completing their case projects. The teachers gather data, determine the students' needs in writing, design and implement a lesson designed to help the student in a particular area of writing, reflect on the lesson, and research an issue related to teaching writing. These elements are then synthesized into a case study as the final product.

The teachers are asked to gather multiple forms of data, including interviews, assessments, and observations, to support their interpretations of the focal student's interests, strengths, and needs in designing their lesson plan. This is how one teacher put this information together in an overview:

> Evidence gathered from student writing samples and the state-mandated writing assessment shows that José has difficulty re-telling events in a sequence. Informal observation of the student at recess tells the researcher that José enjoys baseball. José's responses on a personal interest inventory confirm the observation regarding José's love of baseball and further reveal that José's favorite position is pitcher. The researcher then uses all this data to determine the next step: designing a lesson asking José to write a process essay describing the steps a player must take to pitch a successful no hitter.

The teacher in this scenario used quantitative data from state-mandated assessments. She gathered qualitative information about the student, both formally and informally, in the form of observations and an interest inventory, and used these, along with her own perceptions, to support decisions regarding future lessons. While this is an abbreviated example, it is suggestive of the types of data collection and distillation that are expected of students enrolled in the course.

As the instructor of the course, I observed that one of the teachers' greatest concerns was their general unfamiliarity with conducting a case study. Across four semesters, a consistent theme that arose was the teachers' need for extra guidance, as most had never conducted a case study before. Although forums were set up to discuss the case studies and classmates were paired for mutual support in writing the assignment, it seemed that a further layer of dynamic scaffolding was still needed. Therefore, I decided to include synchronous meetings at key points during the semester with the hope that these would allow a more informal space for the class participants to discuss and try out ideas and to work through concerns together. The immediacy of synchronous sessions would also provide opportunities to reassure students when they were on the right track and to provide guidance if they became stuck in working out their problems.

The Synchronous Meetings

Synchronous meetings were held at two different points in the 15-week course, the first near the start of the course as the teachers were developing research questions and the second prior to planning their lessons, during the eighth week of the semester. This timing was selected because student feedback suggested these particular stages presented the most challenges and therefore might be points at which discussion among the teacher-researchers might be of greatest benefit. The first meeting offered an opportunity for the teachers to identify manageable issues to focus on in their case studies and to develop these into questions, while the second provided more free-form and creative idea sharing.

Before each synchronous meeting, the teachers were invited to sign up for available time slots using an online polling application. This helped ensure that scheduling across multiple time zones and work schedules was as convenient as possible. Two or three different meeting times were then selected based on their responses, and teachers were invited to attend any one of the meetings. At this point, the purpose of the meetings was again shared with the participants in the class. I found that describing the purpose of the meeting both at the point of polling and again prior to the meeting resulted in greater engagement among the students, who appreciated the opportunity to consider the goals of the session before signing up.

As previously noted, the Adobe Connect software offers audio, video, and text chat capabilities. However, teachers were given the option to use the channels with which they felt most comfortable. This decision was made both to ease anxiety and to forestall any potential technology or connectivity problems. The first 10 to 15 minutes of each synchronous meeting were instructor-led to offer additional information or explanation of the topic at hand. For example in the second meeting, which was about lesson planning, teachers were provided with an in-depth description of issues commonly addressed in writing instruction. Although the instructor was the main speaker for these beginning moments, the participants were invited to comment or ask questions via the text chatting function. During the lesson planning meeting, only questions of a technical nature were asked.

Following the content-focused discussion, the class was divided into small groups using the "breakout rooms" feature of the Connect software. Here, teachers engaged in small group discussion about the topic at hand and the instructor circulated among the small groups. In the first meeting, teachers simply shared their findings from the data they had collected. To begin framing questions to guide their project, they discussed other information that might need to be collected and particular challenges that their individual learners were facing. In the lesson planning phase, teachers were invited to give an overview of their learners and their particular writing concerns and discuss how to select focal concerns and how to address these in their upcoming lessons. This conversation provided the best opportunities for dialectical learning, as teachers engaged in dialogue and negotiation about the issues they had encountered in planning and conducting elements of the case study. During this time, the teachers had an opportunity to engage spontaneously in negotiating concerns and issues they might have regarding the planning and implementation of their case studies. This layer of interaction is central to the notion of dialectical learning.

The example in Figure 6.1 is taken from a text-based real-time discussion, the dialectical discussion of participants leads one student, Malcolm, to change his response to a question about the objectives he has been working on with his focal student (all names are pseudonyms).

FIGURE 6.1. I'D LIKE TO CHANGE MY ANSWER

Malcolm:	I would like to help her organize her ideas a bit more as well as work on "flow"
Anne:	Do you focus on global or local objectives? or both?
Malcolm:	more local
Sudipta:	I am still not getting global and local objectives!!
Malcolm:	We deal with more specifics involving what her classes are asking of her
Sudipta:	Anne would you give an example?
Anne:	Sure Sudipta!
Anne:	I suppose global would be like the content of writing and focusing on genre, purpose, "flow," etc.
Sudipta:	It sounds like so far I am limited to local ones
Malcolm:	same here
Anne:	Local would be grammar, usage and mechanics in writing . . . . I think!
Instructor:	Anne, you are right on!
Malcolm:	ah, then I guess I will have to change my answer to global :D

In Figure 6.1, students are discussing their recent lessons with their case study participants. Anne inquires about Malcolm's focus in his lessons, and his initial response is that he has been concentrating on "local" writing concerns. Sudipta asks for clarification, and Anne provides a definition for "global" writing concerns and then for "local" concerns as well. After hearing both explanations, Malcolm changes his response to Anne's question. From this example, we can see that the synchronous meeting provided an opportunity not only for Sudipta to seek help from colleagues, but for Malcolm to reevaluate his own response and revise his understanding of the concepts.

Dialectical discussion is evident in the extract in Figure 6.2 as well. In that example, students are working out what to include in their lesson plans, and Jaclyn mentions planning to use a graphic organizer. Melinda's question sends the group into a discussion about "global concerns" in writing, a topic covered during the instructor-led presentation at the start of the meeting. In the following 10 turns, students and instructor negotiate the meaning of global concerns and finally tie this back to Jaclyn's original lesson plan idea of using a graphic organizer.

Although the instructor tried to anticipate students' needs by explaining the concept of "global concerns" at the start of the meeting, the students later had concerns about the meaning of the term. Therefore, the just-in-time discussion about the topic was necessary to help students feel comfortable with their knowledge of its use. The example demonstrates how students dialectically came to a more developed understanding of one element of the lesson planning assignment. Further, this discussion was facilitated by the

FIGURE 6.2. GRAPHIC ORGANIZERS

Jaclyn:	I was thinking of using a graphic organizer . . .
Melinda:	Hey can you explain the global part . . . .
Emily:	global delt [*sic*] with organization
Jaclyn:	I am not sure emily. That is something we need to be sure to ask [the teacher]
Instructor:	Emily's right . . . Global deals with organization . . .
Jaclyn:	global also deals more with content, genre, where local is more of grammar
Instructor:	Also "meaning" "flow"
Instructor:	questions like "Does it make sense?"
Instructor:	so a global concern for a younger learner might be learning to write in a specific genre (letter writing for example)
Emily:	So graphic organizers would be a good tool to use for the global area of a lesson, right?

instructor's provision of student-centered small group discussion time, which in turn was made possible through the immediacy that the synchronous meetings provided.

Conclusion

Dialectical learning rests on a social theoretical worldview, which claims that learners learn best when engaged in dialogue with others. Coupled with practices that encourage practitioner-initiated inquiry, such as case study research, a dialectical framework for online classes allows students to question, discuss, and develop their understanding of issues they encounter in their practice. Multichannel web-conferencing platforms can provide a space for these conversations to take place. The just-in-time nature (see Chapter 5, "Active Learning Through Just-in-Time Teaching in a Hybrid and Flipped Doctoral Seminar") of the synchronous discussion provides a dynamic layer of scaffolding missing from wholly asynchronous discussion boards, allowing students to develop their understanding of concepts in real time. The class describe in this chapter is just one way these meetings can be used to allow students engaged in practitioner inquiry to participate in the open discussion essential in a dialectical approach to teaching and learning.

R Questions for Further Discussion

1. Dialectical learning is a general framework that might encompass many practices. How does practitioner inquiry fit within this framework? What other practices might fit?

2. The role of instructor as designer is extremely important in creating a successful synchronous meeting experience. How would you plan for effective, inclusive, synchronous learning opportunities in an online meeting, using a multichannel communication platform? Focusing on the following, design a plan for your synchronous meeting:

    a. Scheduling

    b. Activity structure

    c. Technical support

3. Using an online class that you are taking, teaching, or familiar with as a starting place, what assignments or activities might benefit from synchronous discussion time? How can this time be structured for students so that opportunities for dialogue are increased?

References

Anderson, T., Rourke, L., Garrison, D. R., & Archer, W. (2001). Assessing teaching presence in a computer conferencing context. *Journal of Asynchronous Learning Networks, 5*(2), 1–17.

Baxter, P., & Jack, S. (2008). Qualitative case study methodology: Study design and implementation for novice researchers. *The Qualitative Report, 13*(4), 544–559.

Boeher, J., & Linsky, M. (1990). Teaching with cases: Learning to question: New directions for teaching and learning. *The Changing Faces of College Teaching, 42,* 41–57.

Bower, M., & Hellstén, M. (2010). *An institutional study of learning and teaching using web-conferencing.* In Z. Abas et al. (Eds.), *Proceedings of Global Learn 2010* (pp. 4168–4177). Association for the Advancement of Computing in Education. Retrieved from http://www.editlib.org/p/34515

Brown, H. D. (1987). *Principles of language learning and teaching* (2nd ed.). Englewood Cliffs, NJ: Prentice-Hall.

Brown, J. S., Collins, A., & Duguid, P. (1989). Situated cognition and the culture of learning. *Educational Researcher, 18*(1), 32–42.

Calderhead, J., & Robson, M. (1991). Images of teaching: student teachers' early conceptions of classroom practice. *Teaching and Teacher Education, 7*(1), 1–8.

Cochran-Smith, M., & Lytle, S. (2011). Changing perspectives on practitioner research. *LEARNing Landscapes, 4*(2), 17–23.

Creswell, J. W. (2011). *Educational research: Planning, conducting and evaluating quantitative and qualitative research* (4th ed.). Boston, MA: Pearson.

Falloon, G. (2011). Making the connection: Moore's theory of transactional distance and its relevance to the use of a virtual classroom in postgraduate online teacher education. *Journal of Research on Technology in Education, 43*(3), 187–209.

Firth, A., & Wagner, J. (2007). Second/foreign language learning as a social accomplishment: Elaborations on a reconceptualized SLA. *The Modern Language Journal, 91*(1), 800–819.

Garrison, D. R. (2003). Cognitive presence for effective asynchronous online learning: The role of reflective inquiry, self-direction and metacognition. *Elements of quality online education*: *Practice and direction, 4,* 47–58.

Hammersley, M. (1995). *The politics of social research.* London, England: Sage.

Kear, K., Chetwynd, F., Williams, J., & Donelan, H. (2012). Web conferencing for synchronous online tutorials: Perspectives of tutors using a new medium. *Computers & Education, 58*(3), 953–963.

Kershner, R., & Hargreaves, L. (2012). Student teachers' distinctive contributions to research on primary school children's beliefs about knowledge and knowing. *Journal of Education for Teaching, 38*(3), 275–293.

Kramsch, C., & Thorne, S. (2002). Foreign language learning as global communicative practice. In D. Block and D. Cameron (Eds.), *Globalization and language teaching* (pp 83–100). New York, NY: Routledge.

Lantolf, J. P. (2000). Introducing sociocultural theory. In J. P. Lantolf (Ed.), *Sociocultural theory and second language learning* (pp. 1–26). Oxford, England: Oxford University Press.

Lambe, J. (2011). Developing pre-service teachers' reflective capacity through engagement with classroom-based research. *Reflective Practice, 12*(1), 87–100.

Lieberman, A. (1996). Practices that support teacher development: transforming conceptions of professional learning. In M. W. McLaughlin & I. Oberman (Eds.), *Teacher learning: New policies, new practices* (pp. 185–201). New York, NY: Teachers College Press.

McBrien, J. L., Jones, P., & Cheng, R. (2009). Virtual spaces: Employing a synchronous online classroom to facilitate student engagement in online learning. *International Review of Research in Open and Distance Learning, 10*(3), 1–17.

McGuire, C. J., & Castle, S. R. (2010). An analysis of student self-assessment of online, blended, and face-to-face learning environments: Implications for sustainable education delivery. *International Education Studies, 3*(3), 36–40.

Ng, K. C. (2007). Replacing face-to-face tutorials by synchronous online technologies: Challenges and pedagogical implications. *The International Review of Research in Open and Distance Learning, 8*(1), 1–10.

Park, Y. J., & Bonk, C. J. (2007). Synchronous learning experiences: Distance and residential learners' perspectives in a blended graduate course. *Journal of Interactive Online Learning, 6*(3), 245–264.

Paulus, T. M., & Phipps, G. (2008). Approaches to case analyses in synchronous and asynchronous environments. *Journal of Computer-Mediated Communication, 13*(2), 459–484.

Pawan, F., Paulus, T. M., Yalcin, S., & Chang, F. S. (2003). Online learning: Patterns of engagement and interaction among in-service teachers. *Language Learning & Technology, 7*(3), 119–140.

Price, J. N. (2001). Action research, pedagogy and change: The transformative potential of action research in pre-service teacher education. *Journal of Curriculum Studies, 33*(1), 43–74.

Rourke, L., Anderson, T., Garrison, R. D., & Archer, W. (1999). Assessing social presence in asynchronous text-based computer conferencing. *International Journal of E-Learning & Distance Education, 14*(2), 50–71.

Smyth, R. (2011). Enhancing learner–learner interaction using video communications in higher education: Implications from theorising about a new model. *British Journal of Educational Technology, 42*(1), 113–127.

Stahl, G. (2006). *Group cognition: Computer support for building collaborative knowledge (Acting with technology)*. Cambridge, MA: MIT Press.

Stake, R. E. (1995). *The art of case study research.* Thousand Oaks, CA: Sage.

Steed, M., & Vigrass, A. (2011). *Assessment of web conferencing in teacher preparation field experiences.* In M. Koehler & P. Mishra (Eds.), *Proceedings of Society for Information Technology & Teacher Education International Conference 2011* (pp. 2736–2743). Chesapeake, VA: AACE. Retrieved from http://www.editlib.org /p/36729

Sulzer-Azaroff, B. (1995). Behavioristic theories of teaching. In L. W. Anderson (Ed.), *International encyclopedia of teaching and teacher education* (2nd ed.; pp. 96–100). Cambridge, UK: Cambridge University Press.

Toom, A., et al. (2010). Experiences of a research-based approach to teacher education: Suggestions for future policies. *European Journal of Education, 45*(2), 331–344.

Tryggvason, M. T. (2009). Why is Finnish teacher education successful? Some goals Finnish teacher educators have for their teaching. *European Journal of Teacher Education, 32*(4), 369–382.

Vonderwell, S. (2003). An examination of asynchronous communication experiences and perspectives of students in an online course: A case study. *The Internet and Higher Education, 6*(1), 77–90.

Vygotsky, L. (1962). *Thought and language.* (A. Kozulin, Trans.). Cambridge, MA: M.I.T. Press. (Original work published 1934.)

Vygotsky, L. S. (1978). *Mind in society: The development of higher psychological processes.* Cambridge, MA: Harvard University Press.

Wang, C. M., & Reeves, T. C. (2007). Synchronous online learning experiences: The perspectives of international students from Taiwan. *Educational Media International, 44*(4), 339–356.

Yin, R. K. (2003). *Case study research: Design and methods.* Newbury Park, CA: Sage.

CHAPTER 7

Scaffolding in Online Process-Writing Instruction

Faridah Pawan and Jaehan Park

One of the benefits of scaffolding is that it engages

the learner . . . . This gives them more a "can-do"

versus a "this-is-too-hard" attitude.

—*Van Der Stuyf, 2002, p. 11*

Introduction

When it comes to writing, the open-endedness of its nature can be intimidating. We all need courage to proceed! The good news is that the online medium opens up new possibilities for language teacher educators and language teachers alike to support students' writing and to use it as a means to learn. It also facilitates the process approach to writing, where the task is broken down to manageable stages, and makes it easier for collaboration to be a part of scaffolding in the writing process.

One of the main learning objectives of the course described in this chapter is the exploration of global sociocultural issues affecting teaching of English as a foreign language/English as a second language (EFL/ESL) teachers. The teachers in the class undertake different forms of teacher action research involving systematic, intentional, and self-critical inquiry about language teaching in different international settings. To facilitate their successful achievement of this objective, four writing assignments are incorporated into the course design. The writing assignments are not just solitary tasks but are designed to take advantage of the online settings through a scaffolded writing process.

Scaffolded and Process Writing
in the Online Medium

Cheng (2009) points out that although online technologies allow multimodality, the text-only feature available in an online class can be beneficial for student writers because it allows them to focus on writing solely as a means of sharing knowledge and self-expression. In particular, responses from both peers and instructors can help students immediately "see themselves as writers, understand all that is involved in addressing an audience, and see how multifaceted a thing writing in any context really is" (Bruech cited in Cheng, p. 17). The capability to share writing in an online class also gives students a wider sense of audience in that they are not only writing for their instructors but also for their peers, whether near or far.

One of main characteristics of asynchronous (not in real time) online learning is that classroom learning can be flexibly spread throughout the week rather than restricted to fixed time slots (Ally, 2008). In this regard, the medium creates opportunities not always readily available in the face-to-face environment. First, there are multiple occasions for students to showcase their writing in progress, not only to their instructors but also to their peers. This facility in turn creates multiple opportunities for peer and instructor responses (through a variety of online technologies that support audio, video, written, live, and asynchronous feedback) as well as provides a means for everyone in the class to learn from each other. For example, the "multi-versioning" in wikis, in which all draft versions can be archived, and the track changing capabilities in Word, in which all changes can be preserved, allow everyone to trace the evolution of a piece of writing as it progresses toward the version most acceptable to authors and readers alike.

Furthermore, the ease with which reviewers' comments can be saved and archived provides opportunities for students and instructors to examine both past and current feedback. For students, this facility provides opportunities to gain deeper insight, while, as Cheng (2009) notes, instructors can "monitor students' conversations and redirect them to give more specific and critical viewpoints if they find that any individual learner is giving comments that are too superficial or unhelpful" (Cheng, 2009, p. 18).

In this regard, the online medium makes writing more of a dialogue than a mono-logue. In lieu of the cumbersome and time-consuming process of printing out paper copies of writing and giving them to reviewers for feedback, the online medium makes posting papers direct and providing feedback immediate, greatly facilitating the writing and reviewing process. In Google Drive, for example, writers and readers can meet in the margins of the screen (Lee & Schallert, 2008). Once readers have provided written feedback using the comment function, writers can easily add replies. This facility keeps the writing and commenting processes fluid and interactive so that peers and instructors can engage jointly in considering each other's writing, without fear of irrevocably defacing a carefully crafted but static body of work.

There is something to be said also about the "distancing effect" in an online writing class that impacts the quality of comments. Guardado and Shi (2007) report that peers' online comments are more honest and trustworthy. Additionally, instead of focusing on mechanics and structure exclusively, which tends to happen in face-to-face settings, Jones, Garralda, Li, and Lock (2006) report that students in online classes focus more on larger issues such as content and the process of writing itself. Last, the online medium draws more comments from students. Sullivan and Pratt (1996) report 100% participation in making comments online in comparison to 50% participation in face-to-face settings.

Online language courses using discussion forums for peer review also enjoy the benefits of computer-mediated communication (CMC) in providing feedback. CMC, human communication occurring through the use of electronic devices (McQuail, 2005), is known to support students in taking a more active and autonomous role when seeking feedback (Warschauer, Turbee, & Roberts, 1996). One reason for this greater receptivity is the close-knit sense of community that CMC fosters due to frequent interaction. The environment also encourages a sense of group knowledge (Warschauer, 2002) and trust in its value as it is shared by familiar people who share similar struggles and are vested in the same goals.

Hard and Soft Scaffolding as Pedagogical Concepts

Scaffolding is a process that enables to a novice to achieve a goal that would have been impossible without assistance from an advanced peer (Wood, Bruner, & Ross, 1976). Vygotsky's (1978) notion of the zone of proximal development (ZPD) is pivotal to concep-tualizing scaffolding. He described ZPD as "the distance between the actual developmental level as determined by independent problem solving and the level of potential development as determined through problem solving under adult guidance, or in collaboration with more capable peers" (p. 86). Antón (1999) emphasized the value of peer-to-peer scaf-folding, showing how interaction among novices and peers can expand opportunities for scaffolding learning. Online communal writing facilitates both student-student and instruc-tor-student scaffolding by creating online communal space for expert-novice and peer-peer interactions to happen.

Educators have applied the notion of scaffolding in many different ways. Among various applications of ZPD, Saye and Brush's (2002) hard and soft scaffolding is particularly useful in designing online instruction because it helps instructors both to plan lessons in advance and to prepare for support needs that arise spontaneously. Hard scaffolding is the expert guidance embedded in online instruction, which Saye and Brush define as "static supports that can be anticipated and planned in advance based on typical student difficulties with a task" (2002, p. 81). Hard scaffolding provides students with conceptual and strategic roadmaps that help them achieve their learning goals. However, assistance needed for tackling complex conceptual tasks cannot always be anticipated and may require impromptu support from an instructor. Saye and Brush (2002) call this spontaneous support soft scaffolding. Different from hard scaffolding, soft scaffolding is "dynamic and situational" (Saye & Brush, 2002, p. 82) and requires teachers to constantly monitor students' comprehension and provide timely support based on the feedback they receive.

Saye and Brush's (2002) study on teaching history online using hard and soft scaffolding gave us the foundation on which we developed our approach to scaffolding our students' writing using the process approach in an online environment. As hard scaffolding, we addressed such issues as situating evidence within a larger conceptual context and critical reasoning by providing documents, storyboard templates, and model storyboards demonstrating persuasive and dialectical reasoning. For soft scaffolding, we held regular teacher meetings with collaborating groups at various stages of process writing, including gathering data prior to writing, making decisions while writing, and debriefing after the writing task had been completed. Saye and Brush (2002) also suggested that when soft scaffolding becomes routinized to the point at which problems to be addressed can be predicted, teachers may find ways to embed it as hard scaffolding, though this should be undertaken with caution as the benefits of spontaneity and responsiveness may be lost in hard scaffolding, and each kind of scaffolding has its place in the overall process. They argued that whereas strategic thinking skills—for example, taking alternative approaches to decision making (Hannafin, Land, & Oliver, 1999)—can be supported by hard scaffolding, guiding conceptual thinking—such as particular lines of reasoning to consider—requires significant soft scaffolding.

The Process Approach to Writing

The process writing approach places the focus on what the writer does (such as planning and revising with multiple drafts) rather than on what the final product looks like (Hedgcock, 2005). In that regard, Susser (1994) points out that it also involves students' awareness that writing is not simply a process of putting down thoughts on paper but that different types of writing require different processes. He also argues that the approach requires engagement with peers and instructors as "interventionists" and collaborators during the recursive processes of drafting, reviewing, editing, and revising a piece of writing until it is ready to be shared publically.

There are multiple models of process writing with varying steps and stages. As Atkinson (2010) asserts, the role of any model is determined within the sociocultural domain in which the writing instruction is situated, as are the roles and the extent of the influence of writers, peers, and instructors. For this reason, it is important to select a model compatible with the goals and facilities of the instructional setting where it will be implemented. Hughes's model (2007) below provides an illustration of a model of process writing that we consider well suited to an online writing course:

Review provided by classmates as well as the instructor is an inherent part of process writing. Not only do the responses from peer readers help writers improve their texts, peer review itself becomes an excellent learning activity for developing the critical analysis and reading strategies reviewers need to examine their own writing (Lundstrom & Baker, 2009). Despite the benefits of peer review, however, experts in second language writing instruction caution against romanticizing this activity because peer reviewers who lack training are often unable to provide concrete and useful feedback (e.g., Tsui & Ng, 2000;

FIGURE 7.1. WRITING PROCESS BASED ON HUGHES'S MODEL

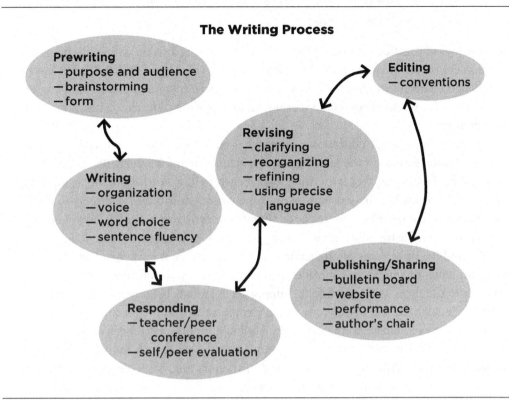

The Writing Process

Note. From *Teaching language and literacy, K–6* by J. M. Hughes, 2007. Retrieved from http://faculty.uoit.ca/hughes/Writing/WritingProcess.html. Copyright 2007 by Janette Hughes. Reprinted with permission.

Mendonca & Johnson, 1994; Leki, 1990). As one approach to such training, Min (2005) has provided guidelines for a four-stage process. First, reviewers ask writers to clarify their intentions for a problematic area of their text ("Are you saying . . . ?"); second, identify the source of the problem from the reader's perspective (for example, a cohesive gap); third, explain the nature of the problem (for example, non-sequitur paragraphs); and finally, make specific suggestions (for example, use key words from the previous paragraph in the thesis sentence of the current paragraph). The sources of information and the frame of reference for peer review can be provided in assignment descriptions, assessment rubrics, and writing examples. It would also be ideal for the instructor to model exemplary reviewer behavior.

In addition to the practical value of peer reviews in the writing process, Hyland and Hyland's (2006) research shows that peer reviews are also interactions at the affective level. Reviewers' acknowledgment of positive aspects of drafts build writers' confidence, increase their motivation, and encourage a sense of investment in their writing.

Pathways to Practice: Hard and Soft Scaffolding in a Writing Pedagogy Course

The pathways of practice we discuss in this chapter are based on an online teacher education course for graduate preservice and in-service teachers of ESL/EFL. The course is conducted completely online and consists of 7 weeks learning and discussion of seven topic areas and 5 weeks of an online writing workshop using different forms of practitioner inquiry.

In this online teacher education course, we used forums, blogs, and wikis. We use online discussion forums in the learning management system for weekly discussions of topics and for facilitating process writing during each writing workshop. Blogs are similar to discussion forums but there usually is only one writer while others can reply to the postings. In our course, blogs are used for students to construct reflective essays on their writing processes. Lastly, wikis are webpages that allow collaborative writing and editing.

We find the three types of applications useful for different purposes. For preexisting hard scaffolding, the mediator-controlled facility of asynchronous forums enables the instructor to use them as a repository of supportive materials before and when they are requested. In addition, the discussions and exchanges stored in the forums can serve as resources as well. Blogs, on the other hand, allow for personal, reflective, and self-expression and thus provide instructors with insight as to what each individual student may need help with. With wikis, students and instructors are able to engage jointly in the development and refinement of ideas and structure in writing. In that regard, wikis can be considered communal soft scaffolding. However, the multi-versioning function of wikis also allows for the changes made by collaborators to be viewed and revisited at any time and in that regard they can also serve as hard scaffolding. Thus, used together, the three applications support students' engagement in writing as a process. Table 7.1 compares the characteristics of the three types of applications based on Miyazoe and Anderson's (2010) work.

The three applications and their uses are an inherent part of the scaffolding of the course, which requires students to complete four writing assignments: contextual autobiography, curriculum analysis, standards deconstruction, and critical incidents experienced. Each assignment uses a different forms of practitioner inquiry, which is research conducted by practicing educators on their particular teaching contexts, focusing on how these contexts shape learning. The class takes a sociocultural approach of understanding human learning as a situated social activity (Johnson, 2006) in that one-third of the content consists of expert knowledge and two-thirds consists of the teachers' knowledge of themselves as learners and their understanding of the schools and schooling contexts in which they teach (Freeman & Johnson, 1998).

The first writing workshop has students writing a contextual autobiography in which they articulate foundational experiences that have shaped their education and reflect critically on their professional journey and the forces that have shaped and sustained them along the way. The second and third writing workshops invite students to deconstruct the English language curricula and standards in the locations in which they are currently

TABLE 7.1. CHARACTERISTICS OF FORUMS, BLOGS, AND WIKIS

	Forums	Blogs	Wikis
Presentation format	Threaded	Reverse chronological	Final product
Authorship structure	Controlled by moderator	Controlled by author	Open
Administrators	One/many	One	Many
Editing	Not allowed/or allowed	By creator	By many
Work mediation	Collective	Individual	Collective
Activity focus	Exchange	Express	Change
Mood-relevant orientation	Cooperative	Individual	Collaborative

Note. Adapted from "Learning Outcomes and Students' Perceptions of Online Writing: Simultaneous Implementation of a Forum, Blog, and Wiki in an EFL Blended Learning Setting" by T. Miyazoe and T. Anderson, 2010, *System, 38*(2), p. 186. Used with permission.

teaching or wish to teach so as to understand the knowledge, skills, and dispositions required as well as the underlying sociocultural agenda that is in place. The final two workshop weeks are reserved for critical incidents (CIs; Cushner & Brislin, 1996). Students draw from their own real-life teaching crises and work backward to identify factors that led up to the crises. The aim is to develop a multilayered understanding of the crises to inform decision making about the next steps and similar experiences rather than to come up with solutions to the crises. (In Chapter 8, "Using the Online Platform as a Third Space for Exploring Cultures and Contexts in EFL Teacher Education," we see how these online autobiographies and critical incidents also became "third spaces").

As mentioned above, the asynchronous and repository nature of the forums is optimum for hard scaffolding. The discussion forum in Oncourse, the learning management system used by the instructors, is introduced at the beginning of the class. Reviewer training sessions take place here, and all discussions and materials are archived for retrieval at students' convenience. The students' writing process begins with both peers and instructors brainstorming as they discuss ideas, explore issues, and argue points. Having been archived, the threaded discussions are available for students to revisit on their own as they consider how to proceed. Instructors scaffold the process by providing resources such as rubrics to help students learn what is expected of them and how to monitor the quality of their own writing. Besides the discussions, the first drafts of papers are also uploaded into the forums so that students can keep track of their writing progress as well as peers' and instructors' comments. Additionally, the forums also contain a question and answer (Q & A) segment, examples from previous students, links to writing support websites such as the Indiana University Writing Tutorial Services or the Purdue Online Writing Lab

(OWL), and links to research journals such as *The Journal of Second Language Writing*. The forum is also a repository of resources contributed and shared by everyone in class.

In our course, blogs are a way for instructors to provide soft scaffolding. Students use them to reflect on the writing process every 3 weeks. Instructors use the blogs to identify students' struggles, which they address directly and individually. While students always have the option of keeping their blog reflections and instructors' responses confidential, if they choose to share them, the reflections can allow all members of the class to identify with their fellow classmates' difficulties and angst without having to articulate their own difficulties. Reading the reflections can also encourage students to express their own feelings and increase opportunities to receive constructive feedback. For similar reasons, the option of making instructors' responses public can be helpful to everyone in the class. Wordpress, Blog.com, and Hubspot are all possible sources for blogging. Additionally, individual learning management systems (LMS) usually have their own blogging facilities.

In a similar way to the forum, the wiki is a collaborative space for peers and instructors to partake in the writing process. When students have posted their work on the wiki, peers and instructors are invited to add information, suggest structural changes, and so on. The wiki archives all the revised versions, and the student authors have the final say as to which version they want to showcase as a final piece. Equally important is that all the writing undertaken in wiki is accumulated into a wikibook format that is publicly accessible. This gives the students an authentic audience for their work, which is essential for motivation. Others who read the wikibook will in turn have the benefit of information related to English language teaching contexts, curricula, and standards around the world. The free wikibook service we use is Wikispaces; there are other free wiki services available including Wikidot and PB Works. Google Sites can also be used for posting students' work in a wiki format.

In addition to strategic use of forums, blogs, and wikis, instructors meet synchronously with each student once a month. As Saye and Brush (2002) point out, face-to-face conferences provide the opportunity to reassure students as to the value of their work and spontaneously address previously unarticulated challenges. In our course, students can choose among various conferencing technologies, including Adobe Connect, Blackboard Elluminate, Google Hangout, and Skype, each of which offers screen share functions so instructors can view and discuss students' writing with them. Besides allowing students to choose a platform with which they are familiar and feel comfortable, instructors also invite students to set their own agenda for the conference (Hewett, 2010). In these ways, responsiveness to students' learning needs and preferences is enhanced.

Importance of Culture in Distant Online Communication

Thorne (2003) has called attention to the need for instructors to clarify the particular cultures for communication in the different technological settings, forums, blogs, and wikis. In this class, blogs are conceived as a venue for informal and self-revealing communications that can be kept private or made public, depending on students' choice. The environment for wikis is the same except for a higher level of formality when students showcase their best work. The forums are behind-the-scenes spaces for open communications that are optimal for collaboration. Thorne demonstrates the importance of common agreement on the culture of use of an application in his example of email dialogues between American university students in California and high school students in France. In discussing the French movie *Le Haine* (The Hatred), a provocative movie on racism, gang violence, and ethnic conflict in a French suburb, the American university students expressed high emotional responses and personal investment in the issues raised by using such typographical cues as exclamation and question marks. In response to the questions from the Americans, the French students focused on the factual accuracy of a comparison between problems in the United States and in France. Frustration resulted in the communications between the two groups because the American students were using CMC as a way to open themselves to closer relationships through mutual concern about a problem that exists in both countries, but the French students were using it as means to engage in factual analysis that created distance between the two parties. Thorne argued that the breakdown in communications that resulted was a consequence of different notions of the culture of use of a computer-mediated platform, in this case, electronic mail. For the Americans, using email evoked a personal style of intimacy outside the expectations of a formal classroom. The French students, who viewed the engagement as an academic activity supported by the Internet-mediated communication, sustained the formality between the two groups. These differences in the cultures of use of email obstructed the co-construction of knowledge as well as development of mutual understanding. It is interesting to note that Thorne (2003) also discussed examples of conversations via synchronous communication (instant messaging), which had the opposite effect as exchanges became more spontaneous and intimate, sometimes resulting in what could be considered instances of hyperpersonalization. In this context, students on both sides shared the same understanding of the culture of the medium and became synchronized in their register of communication as well as in time. This demonstration of the relevance of cultural assumptions underlying uses of different communication media suggest that Dell Hymes's (1972) concept of communicative competence, that is, knowledge of language used by members of a speech community, should be expanded to include understanding the cultures of use of the technological media in which communications take place.

Conclusion

By leveraging the affordances that the new computer-mediated and Internet-supported media offer to facilitate scaffolding and process writing, the online language teacher education course we describe in this chapter emerges as community of practice (Wenger, 1998) for writers in the class. The online medium functions as a venue for process writing, where community members not only engage in writing but also share information and feedback and provide spontaneous assistance, so they are resources to each other in the process. In this way, online communication media and process writing are ideal complements in students' development as writers.

R Questions for Further Discussion

1. In this chapter, we advocate a scaffolded and process approach to writing in an online class. What other approaches and frameworks do you think might work in an online class?

2. What kinds of hard and soft scaffolding have you developed or envision developing for your online writing class?

3. In what ways do you think online hard and soft scaffolding would differ for first- and second-language learners?

4. How might an online writing community of practice differ from that of writers who come together face-to-face?

References

Ally, M. (2008). Foundations and educational theory for online learning. In T. Anderson (Ed.), *The theory and practice of online learning* (pp. 15–44). Edmonton, Canada: AU Press.

Antón, M. (1999). The discourse of a learner-centered classroom: Sociocultural perspectives on teacher-learner interaction in the second-language classroom. *The Modern Language Journal, 83*(3), 303–318.

Atkinson, D. (2010). Extended, embodied cognition and second language acquisition. *Applied Linguistics, 31*(5), 599–622.

Cheng, P. (2009). *Integrating online peer reviews into a college writing class in Taiwan.* (Unpublished doctoral dissertation). Bloomington, IN: Indiana University.

Cushner, K., & Brislin, R. W. (1996). *Intercultural interactions: A practical guide.* Thousand Oaks, CA: Sage.

Freeman, D., & Johnson, K. E. (1998). Reconceptualizing the knowledge-base of language teacher education. *TESOL Quarterly, 32*(3), 397–417.

Guardado, M., & Shi, L. (2007). ESL students' experiences of online peer feedback. *Computers and Composition, 24*(4), 443–461.

Hannafin, M., Land, S., & Oliver, K. (1999). Open learning environments: Foundations, methods, and models. In C. Reigeluth (Ed.), *Instructional design theories and models* (Vol. II). Mahwah, NJ: Erlbaum.

Hedgcock, J. S. (2005). Taking stock of research and pedagogy in L2 writing. In E. Hinkel (Ed.), *Handbook of Research in Second Language Teaching and Learning* (pp. 597–613). Mahwah, NJ: L. Erlbaum.

Hewett, B. L. (2010). *The online writing conference: A guide for teachers and tutors.* Portsmouth, NH: Boynton/Cook Publishers.

Hughes, J. M. (2007). *Teaching language and literacy, K–6.* Ontario, Canada: University of Ontario Institute of Technology. Retrieved from http://faculty.uoit.ca/hughes /Writing/WritingProcess.html

Hyland, K., & Hyland, F. (2006). Contexts and issues in feedback on L2 writing: An introduction. In K. Hyland, & F. Hyland (Eds.), *Feedback in second language writing: Contexts and issues* (pp. 1–19). New York, NY: Cambridge University Press.

Hymes, D. (1972). On communicative competence. In J. B. Pride & J. Holmes (Eds.), *Sociolinguistics* (pp. 269–293). Harmondsworth, UK: Penguin Books.

Johnson, K. (2006). The sociocultural turn and its challenges for second language teacher education. *TESOL Quarterly, 40*(1), 235–257.

Jones, R. H., Garralda, A., Li, D.C. S., & Lock, G. (2006). Interactional dynamics in on-line and face-to-face peer-tutoring sessions for second language writers. *Journal of Second Language Writing, 15*(1), 1–23.

Lee, G., & Schallert, D. L. (2008). Meeting in the margins: Effects of the teacher-student relationship on revision processes of EFL college students taking a composition course. *Journal of Second Language Writing, 17*(3), 165–182.

Leki, I., (1990). Potential problems with peer responding in ESL writing classes. *CATESOL Journal, 3*, 5–17.

Lundstrom, K., & Baker, W. (2009). To give is better than to receive: The benefits of peer review to the reviewer's own writing. *Journal of Second Language Writing, 18*(1), 30–43.

McQuail, D. (2005). *McQuail's mass communication theory*. London: SAGE Publications.

Mendonca, C. O., & Johnson, K. E. (1994). Peer review negotiations: Revision activities in ESL writing instruction. *TESOL Quarterly, 28*(4), 745–769.

Min, H.-T. (2005). Training students to become successful peer reviewers. *System, 33*, 293–308.

Miyazoe, T., & Anderson, T. (2010). Learning outcomes and students' perceptions of online writing: Simultaneous implementation of a forum, blog, and wiki in an EFL blended learning setting. *System, 38*(2), 185–199.

Saye, J. W., & Brush, T. (2002). Scaffolding critical reasoning about history and social issues in multimedia-supported learning environments. *Educational Technology Research and Development, 50*(3), 77–96.

Sullivan, N., & Pratt, E. (1996). A comparative study of two ESL writing environments: A computer-assisted classroom and a traditional oral classroom. *System, 24*(4), 491–501.

Susser, B. (1994). Process approaches to ESL/EFL writing instruction. *Journal of Second Language Writing, 3*(1), 31–47.

Thorne, S. L. (2003). Artifacts and cultures-of-use in intercultural communication. *Language Learning & Technology, 7*(2), 38–67.

Tsui, A. B. M., & Ng, M. (2000). Do secondary L2 writers benefit from peer comments? *Journal of Second Language Writing, 9*(2), 147–170.

Van Der Stuyf, R. R. (2002). Scaffolding as a teaching strategy. Retrieved from http://www.learningace.com/doc/2394100/dfaa039e979d32143dce61be88736768/van-der-stuyf-paper

Vygotsky, L. S. (1978). *Mind in society: The development of higher psychological processes*. Cambridge, MA: Harvard University Press.

Warschauer, M. (2002). Networking into academic discourse. *Journal of English for Academic Purposes, 1,* 45–58.

Warschauer, M., Turbee, L., & Roberts, B. (1996). Computer learning networks and student empowerment. *System, 24*(1), 1–14.

Wenger, E. (1998). *Communities of practice: Learning, meaning, and identity.* New York, NY: Cambridge University Press.

Wood, D., Bruner, J. S., & Ross, G. (1976). The role of tutoring in problem solving. *Journal of Child Psychology and Psychiatry, 17*(2), 89–100.

CHAPTER 8

Using the Online Platform as a Third Space for Exploring Cultures and Contexts in English as a Foreign Language Teacher Education

Jaehan Park, Amber N. Warren,
Kelly A. Wiechart, and Faridah Pawan

Language teachers themselves are multilingual

subjects, with memories, passions, interests, and ways

of making sense of their own and their students' lives.

—*Kramsch, 2009, p. 208*

Introduction

Carefully and responsibly preparing teachers to work in multicultural settings is an important aspect of English as a foreign language/English as a second language (EFL/ESL) teacher education, not least for this preparation's part in the positive spell teachers cast when they acknowledge and encourage each student's potential to learn. Without such preparation, teachers may not examine and interrogate stereotyping, prejudices, and biases in the classroom, making it an unsafe place for some students and detrimental to their learning. Consequently, the magic of teachers' spell in making a difference in their students' lives is compromised.

Typically, this preparation has occurred through field experiences or laboratory situations. However, the research on the effectiveness of these approaches is mixed.

Some studies suggest that even after this preparation, both beginning and experienced teachers may still feel underprepared to work with multicultural populations in their own classrooms (e.g., Polat, 2010; Reeves, 2006). Other findings indicate that the experiences teachers have in their education courses can positively affect their perceptions about working with diverse language learners (Coady, Harper, & de Jong, 2011; Olson & Jimenez-Silva, 2008). One factor in this preparation is teachers' encounters with a variety of language learners. As Schmidt (1998) has pointed out, when teachers "become acquainted with cultural differences through individuals in the culture, there is a significant impact that personalizes and internalizes the experience" (p. 28). The worldwide reach of the Internet may provide opportunities for such encounters.

Global online classrooms can provide opportunities for teachers to interact with colleagues in both close and distant settings and to examine their assumptions about language teaching and learning. Online classrooms offer rich occasions for sharing personal experiences, learning from the experiences of others, and critically reflecting on personal assumptions. Online teacher education opportunities facilitate this in ways that are not possible in traditional teacher education classes bound by the constraints of time and geographic space. The online classroom, therefore, offers an organic "third space" (Bhabha, 1994, p. 36) where teachers from many cultures and a variety of teaching contexts can come together—a site of identity negotiation, a space for acknowledging the "multiple cultural and discursive practices that people draw from to make sense of the world" (Scherff, Singer, & Brown, 2013).

In this chapter, we describe the culturally relevant pedagogical (CRP) practices of online classes for EFL teachers, framed by the notion of third space. Under "Pathways of Practice," we show how the unique affordances of an online learning environment can be leveraged as participants are invited to reconsider their initial boundaries and personal assumptions about culture through CRP practices that encourage introspection, reflection, and multidirectional dialogues.

Understanding Third Space

Initially, Bhabha (1994) conceptualized third spaces as the physical geographic border zones where cultures met. In particular, third space referred to the hybrid of identity and culture that emerged from the imposition of colonial authority over colonized peoples. A third space, therefore, offered a site of resistance—a way for the disempowered to create a space from which to resist authority or incite change. This notion has been appropriated by various disciplines. For example, in media arts it is used to describe a juxtaposition of the virtual and the physical (Packer, 2005) and in sociology in studies of massive online gaming (Oldenburg, 1997). These third spaces are places which are neither home nor work but where informal social life takes place and where "social capital can be acquired and spent" (Steinkuehler, 2005, p. 18). In intercultural education, third space has been defined as a third culture perspective that moves individuals beyond the binary "I and you" or "self and other" in understanding culture and identity to a "new mental and emotional zone" (Finkbeiner, 2006, p. 25). In language education, it has been described as a "third domain" (Kramsch, 1993) in which second or foreign language learners use their insider's view of their first culture and their outsider's view of target cultures to construct identity and cultural understanding in the process of language acquisition. In the virtual space of an online classroom for language teachers, third space, as a theoretical frame, encompasses Kramsch's third domain perspective as a way to acknowledge the "multiple cultural and discursive practices that diverse students living in multiple areas of the world draw from to make sense of themselves and the world" (Scherff, Singer, & Brown, 2013, p. 376). This space, uniquely afforded by the online medium, is a natural venue for the exploration of identity and cultural awareness that is essential in the preparation of future language teachers. Because delving into identity and cultural awareness is a sensitive undertaking, it can result in conflicts due to differences in opinions and understandings. Also, if not undertaken properly, the exploration can result in binary thinking (Finkbeiner, 2006), a stance of "my culture" vs. "others" or "insider" vs. "outsider." Without in-depth cultural insight and a safe environment for multiple perspectives, cultural exploration can result in teaching that is relegated to covering the topics of "food, fairs, and folklore" (Kramsch, Howell, Warner, & Wellmon, 2007, p. 163).

The third space offered by the online medium provides an ideal combination of intimacy and safe distance for exploring identity and culture as expressed in the practicalities of daily life and lived experiences. In this regard, Kramsch (2009) notes, third space is not a realm of "abstract theories or in random flights of fancy, but in the particularity of day-to-day language practices, in, through, and across various languages" (pp. 200–201). Allais (2012) has represented Kramsch's notion as in Figure 8.1.

Thus, Kramsch's conceptualization of third space captures Freire's (1985) view of culture as an interactive process of individuals creating the world around themselves as defined by how they "labor, create and make life choices" (Wallerstein, 1983, p. 5).

The Online Classroom as a Third Space

The online classroom as a third space offers several advantages. It is possible for people to interact while maintaining anonymity if they choose to do so. Indeed, one frequently mentioned benefit of online spaces is the feeling of safety and freedom that this anonymity affords (e.g., Dall'Alba & Barnacle, 2005). This facility is partially due to the technologically mediated environment. As Merryfield (2003) has suggested, the choice of "facelessness" (p. 147) of the online medium can work like a "veil to protect people as they reveal, question, and take risks" (p. 155). Moreover, the anonymity of online spaces offers the potential to explore new modes of identity (Bargh, McKenna, & Fitzsimons, 2002; McKenna, Green, & Gleason, 2002). As Zhao, Grasmuck, and Martin (2008) have suggested, the online environment makes it possible for people to reinvent themselves through the production of new identities.

However, it is important to remember that the online environment is not completely anonymous. For example, participants engage with one another in what are called "anchored relationships" (Zhao, 2006) through institutional affiliation. The identities of members of the class are "anchored" to their institutions, are thus defined, and are

FIGURE 8.1. THIRD PLACE

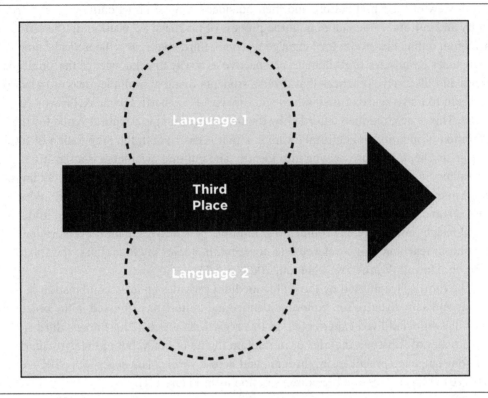

From *Third Place in the French Classroom: A Separate Space for a New Beginning* by L. Allais, 2012. Retrieved from http://blc.berkeley.edu/index.php/blc/post/third_place_in_the_french _classroom_a_separate_space_for_a_new_beginning/. Copyright 2012 by L. Allais. Used with permission.

accountable to not only the rules and policies of the institutions but also their intellectual and cultural norms. Nevertheless, this blend of anonymity and "nonymity" (being known; Zhao et al., 2008) in the online medium creates potential for participants to assume a reflective and critical stance as well as have the option to express provocative ideas within the safety of distance as well as the security of an undefined or assumed identity that may or may not represent their true selves.

As a third space, the online medium also allows for examination of identity and culture in a temporary and conditional environment. The added malleability of technology in online teaching and learning allows students to easily move between private and public discussions and share ideas that can be negotiated and tested before they engage in larger online public spaces such as blogs and wikis. This feature can support students in articulating as well as anticipating difficult conversations and uninformed or naïve judgmental positions, prejudices, and biases, which can predominate in intercultural discussions unless the cultural context is fully understood.

The third space of the online classroom is also a collaborative space (Gutierrez, Baquedano-Lopez, Alvarez, & Chiu, 1999) with classmates who often work and reside around the globe. In this regard, the online classroom is an optimal site for multicultural engagement as it connects students not only from all over the world but also within their immediate context. As mentioned in Chapter 2, "Reflective Pedagogy in Online Teaching," a shared context provides an environment conducive to rich and grounded discussions about identity and lived experiences.

These features of online learning—the choice of anonymity and nonmity, facile movement between private and public reflections, and engagement embedded in the daily lives of students—make the online environment ideal for providing a space for identity negotiation and cultural exploration. These undertakings are important for the professional growth of both preservice and in-service language teachers. As Kramsch (2009) asserted, "language teachers themselves are multilingual subjects, with memories, passions, interests, and ways of making sense of their own and their students' lives" (p. 208).

Pathways of Practice: Multicultural Third Space

In this section, we describe activities in an online class aimed at developing English teachers' global awareness. Participants in the course are typically master's students seeking ESL or EFL licensure. The course lasts 15 weeks and is taught wholly online. Students in the course come from countries around the globe, and the course is designed to take advantage of the variety of teaching contexts and background experiences of the participants. In it, participants explore their personal and teaching identities while investigating central issues involved in global English teaching, such as teaching approaches, English medium instruction, varieties of English, language testing, standards, and curricula. The course takes advantage of the third space afforded by the online medium in considering the controversies around some of these issues. First, the choice of anonymity and nonymity is always available to students, and we include online practices and activities that highlight the potential of this choice. For example, our online students have multimodal options for how to introduce themselves, including photographs, music, artwork, and teaching clips. As the following excerpt suggests, having this choice is essential for the continued participation of all students:

> I do not want my picture to be up. I am a Black woman, a Muslim and I wear a hijab, living in the most conservative part of Florida . . . . Even if I didn't say anything, just a picture of me will trigger all kinds of preconceptions, misconceptions. I want to be able to say things and not to be pre-judged, pre-anything!

We also developed creative approaches to online role play while discussing substantive cross-cultural issues. For example, we have used online chats in an activity in which, taking advantage of online anonymity, students assume made-up roles to discuss an *Atlantic Monthly* article, "The Insufficiency of Honesty" (Carter, 1996), which challenges readers to make a distinction between honesty and integrity. According to Carter, the latter is discerning what is right and wrong, acting on what is discerned even at personal cost, and acknowledging openly that the action taken is based on individual judgment.

Throughout the discussions, students provide culturally based reasons for their positions while keeping their identities anonymous.

Another activity, which capitalizes on the power of the online medium not only to provide anonymity but also to explore culture from the perspectives of those who reside within various cultures, uses wikibooks as an instructional source to problematize teaching. Although there are caveats as to its utility, the advantages of wikibooks include the fact that material is publishable immediately and thus has currency. Furthermore, its contents can be crowdsourced, that is, information is provided and shaped by the contributions of many. Its utility for generating productive discussions among EFL teachers is illustrated by the following chapter of one of our student-composed wikibooks:

> In early summer, I was working as an Assistant Language Teacher (ALT) in Japan. My role was to assist the Japanese Language Teacher (JLT) as we team taught (TT) together. One Junior High School I taught at on Wednesdays, the JLT asked me to arrive at 08:00 AM. This was earlier than my starting time of 08:30, but I complied in the beginning. When I was in the office; however, she was busy and we rarely spoke. Soon enough, I stopped coming early because I did not see the point. Our collaboration consisted of a few minutes speaking before or after each class. Then I would wait for her to let me know if she wanted me to help with an activity or by planning a lesson later in the week. If she asked, I prepared an activity and tried to fax it to her a day or two before class. One week when the JLT asked me to find an activity, I found one that was difficult but I felt could work, and I faxed it to her. When I arrived at school the next morning, I asked her about it, and she said that she understood. We got to the classroom, I gave my explanation in English, then turned to her for the Japanese. She had a blank look on her face. It turned out she didn't understand. I said OK, let's just forget it and move on. She said we couldn't do that, we had to finish because we'd already given them the paper. She changed the activity, said some words in Japanese and the kids did something different than planned, but finished. Back in the office we started talking about what happened. We got into a bit of an argument about what happened. One big part was that I said we should take it back, and she said in Japan we could not do it, and that I didn't understand. This ticked me off, so I said something about how she said she understood the activity but she didn't, then she mentioned how I was often late, and so on and so on. It ended poorly and we barely spoke for the next few weeks. What happened?

The responses the student obtained ranged from the suggestion that there were misconceptions about a shared common reality and a reminder about different cultural levels of comfort with open and verbal confrontations to a verdict that the writer lacked professional development and preparation to serve in the community. All the input the student received contributed to his developing knowledge of how to grow as an U.S. EFL teacher in Japan.

We also used wikibooks to publish the educational autobiographies of the EFL teachers in our class. For the first major assignment, students read published autobiographies written by English language learners, then construct their own "educational autobiographies," focusing on foundational educational experiences and critically reflecting on the forces that have shaped them as current or future educators. The guidelines for these autobiographies are supplied below (see Figure 8.2). Through these autobiographies, we attempted to create a third space or what Finkbeiner (2006) characterized as the "metaphorical leg-room that allows questioning of the self and of the other in a dialogue" (p. 28). Such dialogic cultural explorations through personally invested conversations are aligned with Gay's (2000) CRP principles, whereby the individual's cultural heritages and personal experiences are acknowledged and legitimized. Again, students had the option of publishing these autobiographies anonymously in a wikibook, using the guidelines in Figure 8.2, which were inspired by Braine's (2005) book, *Teaching English to the World: History, Curriculum and Practice.*

The wikibook option of anonymity is critical because, as Sennett (cited in Steinkuehler, 2005) has trenchantly put it, "people are only sociable when they have some protection from each other" (p. 23).

The following excerpts depict the intercultural dialogues in this wikibook that were made possible by the use of pseudonyms. "Jonathan," who was from the United States and living in South America, was considering a career change into teaching English. "Panita" was from Southern California and had been teaching ESL in Ohio. The dialogue that emerged from Panita's autobiography illustrates how the online class provided a safe space to ask questions that might otherwise go unasked. In her autobiography, Panita writes

FIGURE 8.2. EDUCATIONAL AUTOBIOGRAPHY GUIDELINES

→ Detailed description of how key life-educational events have shaped and continue to shape views of learning, teaching, and the educative acts and experiences as a whole

→ Detailed description of how social (e.g., personal encounters, peers, role models), cultural, political, and economic events have shaped and continue to shape learning, teaching, and other educative acts and experiences

→ Detailed description of how ideological and philosophical constructs (e.g., ideas, theories, beliefs) have shaped and continue to shape learning, teaching, and professional educational experiences and practice

→ Detailed description of the reasons why the teaching profession was chosen and the objectives and hopes to be accomplished through the profession

Although my parents were welcomed into America and were financially stable, they still kept within them the pain of leaving their country and family under such a turbulent situation. After we were born, my father was determined to educate us as Americans and not only learn but understand the importance of education. There was a possibility that they might never return to their country; therefore they wanted English to be our L1 language, believing that America would be their newly adopted homeland. Both my parents spoke to us in English but reminded us that even though we were Americans by birth, we were tied to India, Pakistan and Bangladesh by our ancestors. I can still remember my father's pride when speaking about his family's land and the prospects he left behind, while my mother would sadly speak about her family and their ambition for her to further her education and become a doctor or magistrate. Both explained that under West Pakistan, Bangladesh had been a very affluent country, because of their export of jute and natural resources. My father told us that countries fight over land, money and honor, but his country fought over language. He explained to us that language was the honor of the people of Bangladesh, and to dismiss Bengali as the language of the working class, the poor class, was an insult to their honor.

Panita described how languages were an important part of her personal identity formation through her early awareness of their political power. In describing the significance of education in her family, she explains how this has influenced her decision to become a teacher. Recognizing similarities in his own identity development and budding teaching career, Jonathan takes the opportunity to probe these experiences in greater depth:

Jonathan: I did have a couple of questions as I was reading your autobiography. What is the status of your Bengali and Urdu? How did your efforts prevail as you lived in a primarily English environment with learning the languages of your ancestry? Ironically, while many people feel it is the duty of immigrants to learn English, I appreciate those who are able to retain their culture when they arrive in this country (which you have described well as being equal to language).

I would also be curious to know how your identity was affected when you were in Bangladesh. After years of hearing about that culture/life, could you identify with it, or did you feel like a foreigner? How did the locals view you? Did you feel as if people resented the fact that you and your family left as times became difficult? I know for Colombians who left during the hard times, they are not as accepted when they come back; they even have a special word for it... so I am curious as to this region of the world.

Panita: I think the best way to describe my Bengali and Urdu is that I know enough to get by. I was exposed to both languages as a child, since my parents continued to communicate with each other in their native tongues. I can't say that I grew up in a predominantly English environment, since we did have family friends from our country that were also expats who came to

America in the early 70s . . . . When returning to Bangladesh, I was viewed as an American because I spoke Bengali like a foreigner, so I ultimately viewed myself as a foreigner. It was pretty surreal, since I wasn't able to fully assimilate without being noticed.

This interaction shows how the online third space provides a venue for discussing sensitive issues related to cultural beliefs. As we saw earlier, Panita opened the door to personal identity exploration with her initial response to other published autobiographies and continued this quest by writing her own autobiography and responding to Jonathan's questions. This exchange demonstrates how the global online classroom provides space for teachers from different contexts to learn more about others' experiences in various cultures and environments. The online classroom, framed as a third space, extends opportunities for participants to come into their own as cultural beings (English, 2002). Through sharing personal experiences online, participants become more critically aware of both themselves and the world around them.

Conclusion

The benefits of using an online classroom as a third space for increasing cultural awareness and negotiating identity development come with some ethical concerns about privacy invasion. Thus, in our work, we consulted with the university legal office, which informed us that we are within a legally safe domain if we provide options to students to publish or not publish their work and to remain anonymous or to be identified.

Finally, there may be cultural concerns related to sharing personal experiences without face-to-face contact. Merryfield (2003) found that those from oral cultures face difficulty expressing themselves in an online space. As we have mentioned in the chapter on universal design for learning (Chapter 3, "Applying Universal Design for Learning to Inclusive Teacher Education in an Intensive Online Workshop"), students have the option of presenting themselves in multiple modes.

The asynchronous and semi-anonymous nature of the online discussion forum is optimal for multicultural exploration. Unlike brick-and-mortar classrooms, online classrooms more easily preserve multiple stories, and every story has the same chance to be read by others. Experiences that participants initially underwent in isolation become part of a shared knowledge base in a multicultural online third space.

R Questions for Further Discussion

1. In this chapter, we posit that the online medium is ideal for creating a third space for engaging in conversations about culture, but with a caveat that these conversations must be introduced carefully and sensitively. What other challenges do you see in creating a third space in your instructional contexts? And what ways might you find to navigate through those challenges?

2. In this chapter, we discussed the use of wikibooks for autobiographies. How else could wikibooks or other applications be used to create third spaces?

3. As noted above, Gutierrez et al. (1999) identified third spaces as collaborative spaces. To be used collaboratively, a space must combine play and learning, be both informal and formal, and facilitate the formation of relationships. What other prerequisites do you see that would be necessary the space to be used for collaboration? How could the online medium support them?

References

Allais, L. (2012). *Third place in the French classroom: A separate space for a new beginning.* Retrieved from http://blc.berkeley.edu/index.php/blc/post/third _place_in_the_french_classroom_a_separate_space_for_a_new_beginning/

Bargh, J. A., McKenna, K. Y., & Fitzsimons, G. M. (2002). Can you see the real me? Activation and expression of the "true self" on the Internet. *Journal of Social Issues, 58*(1), 33–48.

Bhabha, H. K. (1994). *The location of culture.* New York, NY: Routledge.

Braine. (2005). *Teaching English to the world: History, curriculum and practice.* Mawah, NJ: Lawrence Erlbaum.

Carter, S. (1996, February). The insufficiency of honesty. *Atlantic Monthly,* 74–76.

Coady, M., Harper, C., & de Jong, E. (2011). From preservice to practice: Mainstream elementary teacher beliefs of preparation and efficacy with English language learners in the state of Florida. *Bilingual Research Journal, 34*(2), 223–239.

Dall'Alba, G., & Barnacle, R. (2005). Embodied knowing in online environments. *Educational Philosophy and Theory, 37*(5), 719–744.

English, L. (2002). *Third space: Contested space, identity and international adult education.* Paper presented at the Annual Conference of the Canadian Association for the Study of Adult Education, Toronto, Ontario.

Finkbeiner, C. (2006). Constructing third space: The principles of reciprocity and cooperation. In P. R. Schmidt & C. Finkbeiner (Eds.), *ABC's of cultural understanding and communication: National and international adaptations* (pp. 19–42). Greenwich, CT: Information Age Publishing.

Freire, P. (1985). *The politics of education: Culture, power and liberation.* Westport, CT: Greenwood Publishing Group.

Gay, G. (2000). *Culturally responsive teaching: Theory, practice and research.* New York, NY: Teachers College Press.

Gutierrez, K. D., Baquedano-López, P., Alvarez, H. H., & Chiu, M. M. (1999). Building a culture of collaboration through hybrid language practices. *Theory Into Practice, 38*(2), 87–93.

Kramsch, C. (1993). *Context and culture in language teaching.* Oxford, UK: Oxford University Press.

Kramsch, C. (2009). *The multilingual subject: What foreign language learners say about their experience and why it matters.* Oxford, UK: Oxford University Press.

Kramsch, C., Howell, T., Warner, C., & Wellmon, C. (2007). Framing foreign language education in the United States: The case of German. *Critical Inquiry in Language Studies, 4*(2–3), 151–178.

McKenna, K. Y., Green, A. S., & Gleason, M. E. (2002). Relationship formation on the Internet: What's the big attraction? *Journal of Social Issues, 58*(1), 9–31.

Merryfield, M. (2003). Like a veil: Cross-cultural experiential learning online. *Contemporary Issues in Technology and Teacher Education, 3*(2), 146–171.

Oldenburg, R. (1997). *The great good place: Cafés, coffee shops, community centers, beauty parlors, general stores, bars, hangouts, and how they get you through the day.* New York, NY: Marlowe & Company.

Olson, K., & Jimenez-Silva, M. (2008). The campfire effect: A preliminary analysis of preservice teachers' beliefs about teaching English language learners after state-mandated endorsement courses. *Journal of Research in Childhood Education, 22*(3), 246–260.

Packer, R. (2005). Composing with media: Zero in time and space. *Contemporary Music Review, 24*(6), 509–525.

Polat, N. (2010). A comparative analysis of pre- and in-service teacher beliefs about readiness and self-competency: Revisiting teacher education for ELLs. *System, 38*(2), 228–244.

Reeves, J. R. (2006). Secondary teacher attitudes toward including English-language learners in mainstream classrooms. *The Journal of Educational Research, 99*(3), 131–143.

Scherff, L., Singer, N. R., & Brown, A. (2013). Mentoring "pre" preservice teachers in third spaces. *Teacher Education and Practice, 26*(3), 375–392.

Schmidt, P. R. (1998). The ABC's of cultural understanding and communication. *Equity & Excellence, 31*(2), 28–38.

Steinkuehler, C. A. (2005). The new third place: Massively multiplayer online gaming in American youth culture. *Tidskrift Journal of Research in Teacher Education, 3*(3), 17–32.

Wallerstein, I. (1983). *Historical capitalism.* London, England: Verso.

Zhao, S. (2006). *Cyber-gathering places and online-embedded relationships.* Paper presented at the annual meeting of the Eastern Sociological Society, Boston, MA.

Zhao, S., Grasmuck, S., & Martin, J. (2008). Identity construction on Facebook: Digital empowerment in anchored relationships. *Computers in Human Behavior, 24*(5), 1816–1836.

CHAPTER 9

The Trans-Classroom Teacher

Faridah Pawan and Crystal Howell

We have developed ways of moving through transitions—patterns and behaviors—which have either been generative or degenerative to our development and the formation of our future.

—Liminal Space: Finding Life between Chapters, 2011, para. 10

We started this book with a reference to the movie *The Wizard of Oz*, where a teenager named Dorothy and her dog, Toto, are swept up by a tornado and carried off to the Land of Oz. In Oz she encounters numerous unusual characters—some friends and some foes—and battles the Wicked Witch of the West as she journeys toward the Emerald City, the home of the Wizard of Oz, in order to find a way back to her home in Kansas. At the end of the movie, we find Dorothy waking up at home, where she realizes that her time in Oz has all been a dream, the rather pleasant effect of a bump on the head during a tornado. Whether she is home because she followed the Wizard's instructions—clicking together her magical ruby slippers while chanting, "There's no place like home"—or whether Oz was simply an illusion is immaterial in the film. When she awakens in Kansas, she is a bit wiser, and her world is intact. Her family is safe, and she is content to be home again, an ending that confirms the sentiment that brought her back: "There's no place like home." But in the book *The Wonderful Wizard of Oz* (Baum, 1900), Oz is a real place, not a fantasy. By popular demand, Baum wrote a number of subsequent books in which Dorothy has more adventures and crosses the border between her world and Oz many more times. In the sixth book, *The Emerald City of Oz* (Baum, 1910), Dorothy and her Aunt Em and Uncle Henry go to live permanently in Oz after their farm fails, changing the whole idea of home. Each time Dorothy crosses the border between her world and that of Oz, does she notice that her view of her native world is altered by her experience in Oz and vice versa? How do her trips between her world and Oz change her? What does it mean to have more than one world at one's disposal?

In the new world of online education, we teachers and teacher educators journey back and forth just as Dorothy does: we move from face-to-face instruction to online instruction and back again many times, bringing new knowledge and skills with us on each passage. Lowes (2008) calls this "trans-classrooming" and the teachers, "trans-classroom teachers." The film *The Wizard of Oz* makes the distinction between the familiar and the new in visually arresting fashion. The first several minutes of the film are set in Kansas and are sepia-toned, creating a warm but monochromatic world. When Dorothy opens her front door to look out at Oz, however, she finds herself in an intensely colorful world. The striking contrast between the muted browns of Kansas and the vibrant colors of Oz were all the more striking to early audiences of the film, as it pioneered the use of Technicolor. Sometimes, like Oz, the new world of online education seems unbelievably bright and full of possibility. And other times, just as Dorothy longs to be back in Kansas, we crave the familiarity of a bricks-and-mortar classroom with just our students and a whiteboard. As we make these transitions, do we continue to carry the same beliefs about pedagogy? In this chapter, we explore how well research has answered questions raised by our access to the new world of online teaching and learning, and what questions remain to be pursued.

Nearly two decades since online coursework began to be available for college and K–12 students, our necessary shift in pedagogical thinking is still emerging. As more and more students in K–12 and higher education shift to part- or full-time online coursework, the majority of research related to online teaching has focused on the immediate, practical needs of teachers entering the virtual world of new instructional technologies and struggling to meet the changing needs of their students. For educators moving from teaching face-to-face to teaching fully online or, as is more likely, shifting back and forth between the two modes of instruction, the transition is intriguing but challenging and often frustrating. When they become "trans-classroom" teachers (Lowes, 2005), their teaching foundations may shudder and they may find themselves feeling much like novice teachers—unsure, a bit skittish, but excited and willing to go forward. Ideally, the experience can push teachers toward asking new questions: How do different instructional modes affect learning? How do different modes affect instruction? Do the same pedagogical ideas still undergird practice in both settings? When they return to face-to-face instruction, are they the same teachers or are they changed—methodologically, theoretically, or pedagogically? As more and more teachers experience this transition, generating research to answer such questions will become increasingly critical to the design of teacher education and professional development curricula.

To address questions about the theoretical and pedagogical implications of trans-classroom teaching, we begin with an exploration of "liminal space" (Turner, 1975, p. 13), discuss the major themes that emerged among the studies selected when we used this concept as a conceptual lens, and conclude with pedagogical reflections.

Liminal Spaces: Betwixt and Between

The anthropological concept of liminal space is frequently evoked in discussions of rites of passage from childhood to adulthood as an emotional, intellectual, social, and physical space in which "initiands," guided by "elders," are "betwixt or between all fixed points of classification" (Turner, 1975, p. 232). Derived from the Latin word limen, meaning "threshold," liminal is used by anthropologists to describe spaces where people are in flux, where they are beyond easily classifiable states as they mature, either cognitively, emotionally, or socially. Turner uses the terms *initiand* and *elder* to describe the actors within a liminal space. In education, we more commonly use terms such as *novice* and *expert* to describe students' knowledge and abilities and our role as we guide them toward mastery of particular content or skills. (See Figure 9.1 for other ways to name actors in liminal spaces.) In this space, Turner asserts, it is possible "to contemplate for a while the mysteries that confront all men" (p. 242). The experience of liminality is uncomfortably ambiguous; when situated outside the borders of the known social structure, initiands are confronted with questions—perhaps previously unaskable—and new concepts of identity emerge. Liminal spaces for learners are similarly fraught. Meyer, Land, and Baillie (2010) describe liminality in learning as "a suspended state of partial understanding, or 'stuck place,' in which understanding approximates to a kind of 'mimicry' or lack of authenticity. Insights gained by learners as they cross thresholds can be exhilarating but might also be unsettling, requiring an uncomfortable shift in identity" (p. x).

Cook-Sather (2006) explores the liminality of student teaching within both a traditional setting (her college classroom) and a virtual setting (the email exchanges between the student teachers in her program and their cooperating teachers), thus extending the relevance of liminality to the 21st-century concepts of trans-classroom teaching and trans-classroom pedagogy. The liminal spaces created by Cook-Sather's student teachers existed not *"instead of* the regular time and space in which participants live and move, as it did for Turner's initiands, but rather *in addition to* them" (p. 115). Turner's initiands are exempt from regular time and space; many formalized rites of passage pause all other life events and exist in carefully choreographed physical spaces. Consider, for example, the Jewish bar or bat mitzvah. Although a participant may spend years preparing, the ceremony itself takes only a couple of hours and is typically held in a synagogue. It exists as a brief moment beyond the participant's everyday life. Cook-Sather's student teachers, in

FIGURE 9.1. LIMINAL SPACE AND ITS ACTORS

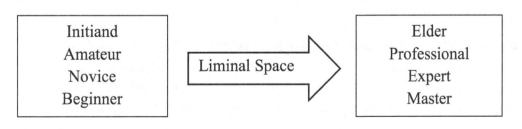

FIGURE 9.2. THE TRANS-CLASSROOM TEACHER'S LIMINAL SPACE

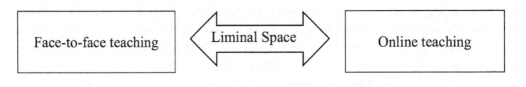

contrast, existed within their liminal space for an extended period of time and while they continued to conduct their normal daily activities. The challenge of the student teachers' liminal experience was exacerbated by its situatedness within everyday life. As modern teachers move between face-to-face and trans-classrooms, they, too, experience a liminal classroom space, just as Cook-Sather suggests her student teachers did. But perhaps more important, these practicing teachers, with already formed beliefs and expectations, experience an even more profound intellectual and professional liminality. Just like Dorothy in the Wizard of Oz books, trans-classroom teachers regularly transgress the traditional map of pedagogical and practical borders. Particularly for highly experienced face-to-face classroom teachers moving to part- or full-time online teaching, transitioning back and forth between initiand and elder status may occur several times as they "contemplate for a while the mysteries" of trans-classroom pedagogy and practice. For trans-classroom teachers, the liminal space is not a frontier to be crossed once and left behind but a zone to be traversed many times as teachers gain trans-classroom expertise.

Trans-Classroom Research: What Do We Know Thus Far?

In this section, we use the liminal space lens to describe five research studies in which the concept of "trans-classroom" (Lowes, 2005) is central. These studies (Baran, Correia, & Thompson, 2013; Downing & Dyment, 2013; Owens, 2012; Lowes, 2005; Torrisi & Davis, 2000) have captured the experiences of teachers transitioning between face-to-face and online instruction and engaging in pedagogical and practical examination of their transition: Table 9.1 (on pp. 124–125) shows the title and authors, purpose (research question), context, methodology, and conclusions for each article.

The major themes that emerged from the articles include revising constructions of pedagogical content knowledge (PCK), reflecting on pedagogical choices, and evaluating preparation for trans-classroom teaching.

Revising Constructions of Pedagogical Content Knowledge

In the research articles we studied, teachers engaged in reexaminations of pedagogical content knowledge, that is knowledge of the subject being taught combined with knowledge of how to teach that content (Shulman, 1987). These teachers' shifting constructions were evident primarily in their successfully revised instructional methods or, where this effort failed, their articulation of a need for new pedagogical thinking. Their reexaminations occurred both while preparing for and teaching online and when they returned to face-to-face instruction.

In both online and face-to-face settings, Lowes (2008) focused deliberately on trans-classroom teachers' instructional choices. For Virtual High School (VHS) teachers, these changes were related to modifying or adding reflective individual assignments such as requiring a peer review activity and overhauling curriculum design using principles of backward design learned in VHS's professional development courses for online teaching. In large and small ways, The VHS teachers' instructional changes demonstrated their ability to consider and execute new best practices in teaching their content areas. The teachers profiled by Baran et al. (2013) were exemplary in part because of their ability to select carefully from the instructional methods with which they had been successful in their face-to-face courses to produce similarly successful outcomes in the online classroom. While Baran et al. do not discuss the teachers' instructional methods upon returning to face-to-face instruction, the teachers' ability to modify face-to-face content and instructional methods indicates that their construction of PCK was flexible enough to accommodate the different pedagogical requirements of the trans-classroom. In forms overt and subtle, trans-classroom teachers' reexamination of decisions about instruction was an indication of their fluid understanding of PCK.

Many of the trans-classroom teachers described by Owens (2012), on the other hand, exhibited a belief and practice disjuncture. For example, her subjects' highest mean score was on the belief question related to interactive teaching, which indicates that most of the teachers in her study recognized the importance of interactivity for online classrooms. However, the corresponding practice question had the lowest mean score; that is, few teachers were actually incorporating interactive instructional methods into their courses. For these teachers, PCK modification was occurring intellectually: they recognized and could identify effective online instructional techniques but could not yet put them into practice. Similarly, most of Torrisi and Davis's (2000) subjects were stalled in an identical position. They could clearly articulate the key competencies students might gain using materials available online in their subject area, yet their stated intended uses of the online materials, as documented in their syllabi, were minimal. Nevertheless, their ability to thoughtfully consider the value of instructional methods beyond those used in their face-to-face classrooms indicates the beginnings of PCK reconstruction.

Downing and Dyment (2013) studied teacher educators who were piloting preservice teachers through the deconstruction and rebuilding of the preservice teachers' PCK. They engaged in an interrogation of whether or not these two processes could be successful without the "organic" (p. 105) interactions that might occur in a solely face-to-face environment. However, the fact that they did not simply dismiss online teaching as ineffective for this purpose and considered online teaching in tandem with onsite teaching indicated that both the educators and their preservice teachers were informed about the possibilities and challenges of trans-classroom teaching and were looking for ways to make it work.

TABLE 9.1. SELECTED ARTICLES FOR CRITICAL ANALYSIS ®

Article	Research questions and purpose	Context	Methodology	Conclusions	
"Tracing Successful Online Teaching in Higher Education: Voices of Exemplary Online Teachers" (Baran, Correia, & Thompson, 2013)	"(1) What are the successful practices that exemplary online teachers employ in their online teaching? (2) How do exemplary onsite teachers make a transition to online teaching in such a way that they create successful practices?" (p. 1).	The context was a large research university in the Midwestern United States.	Research methodology was a multicase study; contextual information and nominations for exemplary teachers were collected via semistructured interviews with six program coordinators; data were collected from ethnographic interviews with six exemplary online teachers.	Teachers' successful practices were linked to their changing notion of their teaching identity when they moved to the online medium. "Programs that prepare faculty to teach online may need to encourage teachers to reflect on their past experiences, assumptions, and beliefs toward learning and teaching and transform their perspectives by engaging in pedagogical inquiry and problem solving" (p. 2).	
"Teacher Educators' Readiness, Preparation, and Perceptions of Preparing Preservice Teachers in a Fully Online Environment: An Exploratory Study" (Downing & Dyment, 2013)	The purpose of the study was to examine how education faculty beginning to teach in a completely online degree program for preservice teachers understood their own pedagogical transition to teaching online generally while also examining the specific implications of online teacher preparation programs.	The context was a midsized Australian university, one year after it began a fully online teaching degree program.	Data were gathered with a 34-question survey (including closed and open-ended questions) completed by 27 teachers.	The participating teachers with extensive onsite experiences initially lacked "confidence and competence with the technological and pedagogical skills required to teach online," but this abated over time with appropriate support. The teachers' apprehension about the appropriateness of the media for the subject was revealed, and issues of teacher identity and teacher pedagogy were "unpacked" (p. 106).	

Article	Research questions and purpose	Context	Methodology	Conclusions
"Online Teaching and Classroom Change: The Impact of Virtual High School on Its Teachers and Their Schools" (Lowes, 2005)	The purpose of the study was to explore the transformation of teachers and their courses as they prepared to teach online and "the two-way interactions, or flow, between face-to-face teaching and online teaching" (p. 1).	The context was virtual high school (VHS), the oldest U.S. provider of distance learning courses.	First, six current and former VHS teachers were interviewed; using data from the interviews, Lowes then developed an online survey completed by 215 current and former VHS teachers.	The results suggest (rather than definitively demonstrate) that online teaching can positively affect face-to-face teaching.
"Hitting the Nail on the Head: The Importance of Specific Staff Development for Effective Blended Learning" (Owens, 2012)	The purpose of the study was "to assess the nature of teaching practices when using [online learning environments in higher education] and to determine whether this practice is aligned with teachers' pedagogical beliefs" (p. 390).	The context was 54 higher education institutions in the United Kingdom.	The author used a 36-question double survey accessed via Survey Monkey; each survey had 18 questions related to pedagogical beliefs and 18 corresponding questions related to teaching practices; data were collected from 529 academic staff respondents.	"The survey found a considerable difference between university lecturers' reported pedagogical beliefs developed while teaching face-to-face, and their actual practices when teaching online and concludes that online learning environments are rarely used effectively to promote student learning" (p. 389).
"Online Learning as a Catalyst for Reshaping Practice—The Experiences of Some Academics Developing Online Learning Materials" (Torrisi & Davis, 2000)	The purpose of the study was to explore the experiences of university lecturers as they designed and developed materials for their university's flexible learning initiative.	The context was Griffith University (GU), Australia.	Ten GU academics were interviewed on three campuses from a cross section of schools including information technology, human services, music, arts, business, and nursing; interviews were 60–90 minutes and organized into four sections (background, preconceptions, experiences during development, and reflection).	Staff developers should provide greater support for academics shifting to online teaching by helping them create spaces where students can be more actively engaged, by recognizing the transition to online teaching expertise as a continuum of onsite teaching, by addressing academics' concerns, by providing interdisciplinary contextualization of new technologies, by promoting a collaborative approach, by fostering reflection, and by providing opportunities to develop basic computer skills.

Reflecting on Pedagogical Choices

Interestingly, the two studies where the theme of reflexivity is present are Lowes (2008) and Baran et al. (2013); these studies include the more experienced and more effective trans-classroom teachers. Determining the amount and kinds of reflection in which teachers engage is difficult in both face-to-face and trans-classroom settings, yet the two studies indicate that reflexivity is an essential component of the trans-classroom liminal space. This is evident in the participants' responses to the open-ended questions in Lowes's study. All the topics represented in Lowes's survey questions elicited responses that demonstrated thoughtful pedagogical decision making, and the teachers themselves frequently cited their trans-classroom (i.e., liminal) position as the factor that allowed them to look more carefully at their practice. The pattern is repeated in participants' responses cited by Baran et al., which indicated a high level of reflexivity. Thus, as trans-classroom teachers struggle and grow within the liminal space, reflexivity becomes a conscious, concentrated professional activity.

Evaluating Preparation for Trans-Classroom Teaching

In the five selected studies, preparedness for the trans-classroom is addressed in two primary ways. Owens (2012) and Downing and Dyment (2013) specifically and overtly address teachers' technological and pedagogical preparation for trans-classroom teaching. By comparing training, certification or licensure, and experience, Owens (2012) finds that the most effective trans-classroom teachers are those who have gained skills through formal education and practice.

But Downing and Dyment found that most new online teachers felt neither confident nor competent in this role. Downing and Dyment's subjects were also reluctant to integrate their face-to-face classroom pedagogical skills with those needed in the online classroom, thus further downgrading their feelings of preparedness. Such uncertainty may change only with more time and experience within the trans-classroom space, as teachers' feelings of inadequacy motivate them to reconstruct their PCK to encompass new media. The success of this process is also linked to the support teachers receive during the transition from a face-to-face classroom to an online classroom. Across the studies, there is a connection between access to individualized, personal support during the initial period of transitioning to online teaching and teachers' evolving online PCK.

Despite a wealth of literature that indicates the importance of technology skills for online teachers (e.g., Bolliger & Wasilik, 2009; Wolf, 2006; Wilson, 2004), Downing and Dyment (2013), Owens (2012), and Torrisi and Davis (2000) all cited online teachers' frustration with the technological aspects of their classrooms. Adequate technological skills are a prerequisite for achieving the level of PCK teachers enjoyed in the face-to-face classroom. In Lowes's (2008) model, these skills as well as online teaching pedagogy are addressed in the professional development courses teachers must take before teaching a VHS course. Hence, for trans-classroom teachers, technology skills and pedagogical content skills are permanently intertwined, and the successful reconstruction of PCK depends on gaining technological competence.

Pathways of the Trans-Classroom: It's a Horse of a Different Color!

Throughout this book, we have showcased the pedagogical stances we take in online teaching and the pathways of practice that emerge from those stances. It is clear that the origins of both are from our work in face-to-face classrooms. However, the four coauthors of this book are also trans-classroom instructors who continue to develop new pedagogical insights and practices as we gain experience. As we reflect on this development, we emerge with a few nascent perspectives that will continue to affect our pedagogical stances and our teaching as onsite and online instructors.

As discussed in Chapter 1, "Teaching Presence in Online Teaching," we distinguish "teacher presence" from "teaching presence." We consider the latter to be gaining increased importance as today's students' learning is mediated by technology whether or not they are in our classrooms. To capture this emphasis, we have set up our instruction so that students will have autonomy as well as guidance while engaged in learning. This prioritizing results in two significant consequences. First, instructors engage in heavy frontloading of preparation before activities begin so that students can find their own way to achieve class goals. For example, face-to-face class discussions, particularly for graduate students with experience in seminar settings, require little explicit instruction from the course instructor. Even experienced students, however, may find online discussion threads challenging to navigate. Establishing discussion protocols can support richer online discussions. While spontaneity and open-endedness remain important, students are supported within the structure that we provide as instructors. Second, we also see division between in-class and out-of-class-learning as unnecessary and counterproductive. Our concepts of teaching and learning extend beyond time and space and whether or not we are present, in person or virtually, in the classroom. This blurring of lines occurs, for example, when interactions in the onsite classroom are continued in the online discussion forums and vice versa, as we described in Chapter 4, "Connectivism and Professional Development Across Large Groups." We concur when our students refer to our online as well as onsite classes as weeklong rather than on specific days.

Although we provide the scaffolding of a clear structure, we strongly advocate fluidity of resources, a value that has grown during our experience as online instructors. Easy and immediate access to online resources allows us to be responsive to students' interests. Also in terms of resources, we expect students will contribute to them as well as participate in developing the course agenda. For example, we label our onsite and online syllabi as "living" documents so materials, and by extension topics, can be added.

Our assessment perspective has also changed. What we have learned from our online experience is that alternative assessment that is deeper and more comprehensive than discrete-item standardized assessment is now within our reach. Technology and the online medium enable us to evaluate active engagement through conversations and collaboration, personal reflections, and growth over time, capturing processes as well as outcomes. At the same time, our face-to-face experience of observing students reminds us that learning can take place even without overt interaction and engagement (Duffy & Kirkley, 2004).

Outwardly quiet students have often demonstrated intellectual involvement through their writing and private conversations with us, showing that despite their classroom reticence, they were engaged through reading and close attention to in-class discussions. However, especially for these students, the online medium is a viable avenue for them to express themselves without the pressure of spontaneity and without the glare of direct attention. Given that we are in an era of social media and 21st-century skills, in which collaboration is seen as essential, our assessment should reflect the current realities of how we work and what we have available as a learning culture. We are therefore at a point of readiness for participatory assessment (Hickey, Honeyford, Clinton, & McWilliams, 2010), in which multiple stakeholders design the assessment and are informed through multimodal means and levels.

Accordingly, our view of the student body has also changed. It is no longer a static population in a specific institutional location but includes those who are near and far and those who are physically present and those who are virtually present and those who are present at the moment or in delayed time, all of which are feasible due to computer-mediated communication. It is also interesting to note that, because of around-the-clock-and-calendar connectivity, at times we feel that we have a closer relationship with our online students than with those we see only at designated times. Paradoxically, the distance accommodated by the online medium results in communications that are more spontaneous and uncircumscribed by scheduled time, an authenticity often not possible in traditional class settings. At the same time, true to the principle of the trans-classroom, we have also used the online medium to obtain a more comprehensive understanding of our onsite students and to improve communication as well as connection with them.

We are also aware of the changing views that students have of us as instructors who, inevitably, still maintain authority. However, they become aware that instructors, as much as students, are "constructed knowers" rather than "absolute knowers" (Belenky, Clinchy, Goldberger, & Tarule, 1986). Together, we are all engaging in the constant process of "construction, deconstruction and reconstruction of knowledge" (Love & Guthrie, 1999, p. 26). Thus, scaffolding this process is one of our defining roles as instructors, although our perception of this role is our own. For some in the field of second language and foreign language teaching, scaffolding means helping students who are ripening or ready to launch to the next level (Johnson, 2009); helping all students undertake a task; and assisting students as they proceed, with or without a knowledgeable other or a novice peer (Lantolf, 2000). On our part, we consider scaffolding a process in which instructors initiate curiosity in learners and provide a meaningful context, useful tools, and a creative but supportive environment in which students negotiate their own terms of engagement and decide where and how to showcase their outcomes to an audience that includes not only instructors but others of their choosing. As metaphorical wizards, we instructors bring together the necessary components for learning, but the students themselves control how to make their own magic and how to use it, with results that are always unexpected and enchanting!

Finally, in this second decade of the new millennium, we accept that it is an accomplished fact that technology, which among many benefits has brought about the online medium, is no longer assistive but inherent in teaching and learning. It is no exaggeration to say that it has created a paradigm shift by expanding the Vygotskian-inspired precept that learning is a social process to apply to teaching. Both are social processes in a dynamic, mutually supportive relationship.

Reflections and Conclusion

As trans-classroom teaching becomes more and more the norm rather than the exception, our understanding of relevant pedagogy must expand, and that expansion must move toward recognizing and exploring the heretofore unacknowledged but critical liminal space trans-classroom teachers occupy. For learners, teachers, and teacher educators, this liminal space, as we write in the beginning of this chapter, can feel turbulent. Our identities and our ways of knowing and doing even the simplest tasks shift. When we first began writing this book, we set out to describe our own experiences as trans-classroom teachers and to link those experiences to the most current research in online education and sound pedagogical practices for creating effective teaching presence in virtual classrooms. We hope that our efforts in this book will embolden our colleagues to take on the role of trans-classroom teachers rather than to avoid it. We have entered into a world of new instructional realities and settings, but we are not unequipped. We have begun to explore this world here, and we hope that researchers and practitioners alike continue to explore it. As we move beyond traditional face-to-face classrooms, we remember Dorothy's exclamation to her dog, Toto, when they first arrived in Oz: "I have a feeling we're not in Kansas anymore!"

R Questions for Further Discussion

1. In this chapter, we reviewed research that explored experiences of trans-classroom teachers. Were the experiences of trans-classroom teaching similar to your own experience? If not, how were they different?

2. As a teacher educator, what are the strategies you have developed to facilitate your preservice and in-service teachers' transition to trans-classroom teaching?

3. Students of teacher education courses often consist of both those who have been using technology from very early in their lives, also known as digital natives, and those who learned to use technology, also known as digital immigrants. Did you perceive any differences in preparedness for trans-classroom teaching between the two groups? Do you see a need to differentiate approaches in facilitating learning to teach for the two groups?

References

Baran, E., Correia, A., & Thompson, A. (2013). Tracing successful online teaching in higher education: Voices of exemplary online teachers. *Teachers College Record, 115*(3), 1–41.

Baum, L. F. (1900). *The wonderful wizard of Oz.* Chicago, IL: George M. Hill.

Baum, L. F. (1910). *The Emerald City of Oz.* Chicago, IL: Reilly & Britton.

Belenky, M. F., Clinchy, B. M., Goldberger, N. R., & Tarule, J. M. (1986). *Women's ways of knowing: The development of self, voice, and mind.* New York, NY: Basic Books.

Bollinger, D., & Wasilik, O. (2009). Factors influencing faculty satisfaction with online teaching and learning in higher education. *Distance Education, 30*(3), 383–397.

Cook-Sather, A. (2006). Newly betwixt and between: Revising liminality in the context of a teacher preparation program. *Anthropology & Education Quarterly, 37*(2), 110–127.

Downing, J., & Dyment, J. (2013). Teacher educators' readiness, preparation, and perceptions of preparing preservice teachers in a fully online environment: An exploratory study. *The Teacher Educator, 48*(2), 96–109.

Duffy, T. M., & Kirkley, J. R. (Eds.). (2004). *Learner-centered theory and practice in distance education: Cases from higher education.* New York, NY: Routledge.

Hickey, D. T., Honeyford, M. A., Clinton, K. A., & McWilliams, J. (2010). Participatory assessment of 21st century proficiencies. In V. J. Shute & B. J. Becker (Eds.), *Innovative assessment for the 21st century: Supporting educational needs* (pp. 107–138). New York, NY: Springer.

Johnson, K. E. (2009). *Second language teacher education: A sociocultural perspective.* New York, NY: Routledge.

Lantolf, J. P. (2000). Second language learning as a mediated process. *Language teaching, 33,* 79–96.

Liminal Space: Finding Life Between Chapters. (2011). *What is a liminal space?* Retrieved from http://inaliminalspace.com/about/what

Love, P. G., & Guthrie, V. L. (1999). Women's ways of knowing. *New Directions for Student Services, 88,* 17–27.

Lowes, S. (2005). *Online teaching and classroom change: The impact of Virtual High School on its teachers and their schools.* Unpublished manuscript, Institute for Learning Technologies, Teachers College, Columbia University, New York, New York. Retrieved from http://www.academia.edu/1106534/Online_teaching_and_classroom_change_The_impact_of_Virtual_High_School_on_its_teachers_and_their_schools

Meyer, J. H. F., Land, R., & Baillie, C. (Eds.). (2010). *Threshold concepts and transformational learning.* Rotterdam, The Netherlands: Sense Publishing.

Owens, T. (2012). Hitting the nail on the head: The importance of specific staff development for effective blended learning. *Innovations in Education and Teaching International, 49*(4), 389–400.

Shulman, L. (1987). Knowledge and teaching: Foundations of the new reform. *Harvard Educational Review, 57*(1), 1–22.

Torrisi, G., & Davis, G. (2000). Online learning as a catalyst for reshaping practice—the experiences of some academics developing online learning materials. *International Journal for Academic Development, 5*(2), 166–176.

Turner, V. (1975). *Dramas, fields, and metaphors: Symbolic action in human society.* Ithaca, NY: Cornell University Press.

Wilson, G. (2004). Online interaction impacts on learning: Teaching the teachers to teach online. *Australian Journal of Educational Technology, 20*(1), 33–48.

Wolf, P. (2006). Best practices in the training of faculty to teach online. *Journal of Computing in Higher Education, 17*(2), 47–78.

Glossary

R

Accessibility — the degree that a technology is able to be accessed by a wide variety user.

Active learning — being actively engaged in the knowledge construction and acquisition process rather than passively listening to one-way lectures. Much of students' preparation takes place outside class so that they are well-informed to take part in class activities, which generally involve collaboration, cooperation, and problem solving.

Advocacy for English language learners — a teacher's action stance explained by Athanases and Martin (2006) as "casting all aspects of school as problematic rather than given" (p. 628) and using one's own expertise to confront issues encountered by students rather than merely relying on others to intercede on the students' behalf.

Asynchronicity — time differential in an online discussion forum, which gives the individual the ability to connect, interact, and think along with others independent of time and space.

Case study research — a form of practitioner inquiry that engages practicing (or soon-to-be-practicing) teachers in classroom-based study of a particular issue or case.

Connectivism — a new learning theory first articulated by Siemens (2004). In connectivism, knowledge is conceptualized as the act of forming and engaging in networks with other learners, organizational knowledge, and stored information.

Connectivity — virtually unlimited interactions of multiple parties in multiple directions in an online medium.

Critical incidents (CI) — brief descriptions of situations in which misunderstanding or conflict arises because of the cultural differences of the interacting parties. CI is frequently used for training intercultural workers.

Critical reflection — the highest level of reflection in Van Manen's (1977) model. At this level teachers question all aspects of the status quo as they reflect on issues of justice and equity in instruction.

Dialectical theory of learning—a perspective that acknowledges social interaction as a necessary condition for learning. Discussion and reasoning are means of knowledge development.

Flipped classroom—instead of a venue for one-way lectures, the classroom is a space where instructors and students work in tandem, co-constructing knowledge through collaborative, cooperative, and problem-solving activities.

Heterarchical Learning—learning viewed in terms of "perspective" rather than "objective" stances and demonstrating growth in students' intellectuality rather than their acquisition of knowledge. It focuses on connections among ideas within an overall goal or vision rather than on their hierarchical ranking from simple to complex.

Hybrid classroom—one where instruction and student participation are both online and face-to-face. "Blended classroom" is another term often used to describe this type of classroom.

Inclusive education—an approach to compulsory education in which all learners are welcomed into all class settings. In fully inclusive learning environments, there is no distinction between "general" and "special" education classes.

Just-in-time teaching (JiTT)—instruction designed to scaffold active learning rather than prescribe what is to be learned. An essential element is the feedback loop (Novak, Patterson, Gavrin, & Christian, 1999) whereby, instead of focusing on knowledge transfer, instructors engage and interact with students, exploring ideas, seeking answers to questions, and co-constructing knowledge based on students' input derived from materials they have read, activities they have engaged in, and problems they have encountered before and while in class.

Learning management System—software application suite for design and delivery of e-learning initiatives.

Liminal space—From Turner's (1975) work in anthropology, an emotional, social, and physical space where "initiands," guided by "elders," exist "betwixt or between all fixed points of classification" (p. 232). Within education, the student teaching experience may be classified as such a space, as is the period when trans-classroom teachers move between face-to-face and online teaching.

Media—tools used to store and disseminate information (e.g., film, newspaper, books, magazines, radio, television, software).

Mentorworking—often used to describe workplace mentoring by more experienced colleagues and/or superiors, extended to the collaborative nature of socioconstructivist teacher education.

Metacognition—mental activity characterized by Jacobs and Paris (1987) as (a) self-appraisal of cognition and (b) self-management of thinking. The former refers to "the static assessment of what an individual knows about a given domain or task" and the latter to the "dynamic aspects of translating knowledge into action" (pp. 258–259).

Mode—culturally and socially constructed ways in which meaning is encoded (e.g., gesture, gaze, posture, music, smell, taste, touch, writing, layout, speech, graphics).

Multi-channel web-conferencing—web-based software that provides multiple means of communication (e.g., video, audio, text) for participants engaged in real-time (synchronous) communication and collaboration.

Pedagogical content knowledge (PCK)—knowledge of the subject being taught (content knowledge) combined with knowledge of how to teach that content (cf. Shulman, 1987).

Practical Inquiry Model (PIM)—operationalized from Garrison, Anderson, and Archer's (2000) conceptualization of the community of inquiry framework, PIM is predicated on sustained reflective discourse through the cyclical stages of puzzlement, exploration, integration, and vicarious/real-life application of understandings (Garrison, 2007).

Practical theory of teaching—as defined by Eylon (2000), an integrated theory of teaching that evolves from the day-to-day experiences of teaching and living in the classroom.

Practitioner-initiated research—also known as practitioner inquiry, the practice of engaging preservice and in-service teachers in research involving learners in the settings in which they practice.

Purdue University's Online Writing Lab (OWL)—houses resources and instructional material related to writing including general writing, research and citation, teaching and tutoring, subject-specific writing, and ESL.

Reflective teaching—an approach that involves teachers' self-evaluation of their practical theories, by means of which they subject their personal beliefs about teaching and learning as well as their teaching practices to critical analysis.

Relational stance—a view that emphasizes connection and understands that learning takes place in relation to others and to the learning resources.

Social presence—defined by Short, Williams, and Christie (1976) as the "saliency" or the mutual noticeability of interlocutors, or communicators, and the consequences of that noticeability; can be understood as the projection of personal characteristics into the online community, or classroom.

Socioconstructivism — applied to education, this theory views teaching and learning as social and scaffolded processes that emphasize students taking control of their own learning and engaging in "curriculum methods and materials designed to allow students to apply concepts being learned to real-world contexts, build local and global communities of practice, and allow opportunities for learning in and out of the classroom" (Huffaker & Calvert, 2003, p. 326). Throughout, teachers and other mentors provide consistent support for students.

Teacher presence — the physical presence of the teacher in the classroom; it is subsumed in the concept of teaching presence in online education.

Teaching presence — "the design, facilitation, and direction of cognitive and social processes" (Anderson et al., 2001, p. 5).

Text-to-speech (TTS) — a type of speech synthesis in written text is translated into audio formats. The converse would be speech-to-text programs, which convert spoken language to written (text).

Third space — a site of identity negotiation, a space for acknowledging the "multiple cultural and discursive practices that people draw from to make sense of the world" (Scherff, Singer, & Brown, 2013).

Trans-classroom teacher — a term coined by Lowes (2008) to describe a teaching move from face-to-face to online teaching, from online teaching to face-to-face teaching, or between the two simultaneously.

Wikibook — an online book created on wiki, a web application that allows people to add, change, and delete content in collaboration with others.

References

Anderson, T., Rourke, L., Garrison, D. R., & Archer, W. (2001). Assessing teaching presence in a computer conferencing context. *Journal of Asynchronous Learning Networks, 5*(2), 1–17.

Athanases, S. Z., & Martin, K. J. (2006). Learning to advocate for educational equity in a teacher credential program. *Teaching and Teacher Education, 22,* 627–646.

Eylon, B. S. (2000). Designing powerful learning environments and practical theories: The knowledge integration environment. *International Journal of Science Education, 22*(8), 885–890.

Garrison, D. R. (2007). Online community of inquiry review: Social, cognitive, and teaching presence issues. *Journal of Asynchronous Learning Networks, 11*(1), 61–72.

Garrison, D. R., Anderson, T., & Archer, W. (2000). Critical inquiry in a text-based environment: Computer conferencing in higher education. *The Internet and Higher Education, 2*(2–3), 87–105.

Huffaker, D. A., & Calvert, S. L. (2003). The new science of learning: Active learning, metacognition, and transfer of knowledge in e-learning applications. *Journal of Educational Computing Research, 29*(3), 325–334.

Jacobs, J. E., & Paris, S. G. (1987). Children's metacognition about reading: Issues in definition, measurement, and instruction. *Educational Psychologist, 22*(3–4), 255–278.

Lowes, S. (2008). Online teaching and classroom change: The trans-classroom teacher in the age of the Internet. *Innovate, 4*(3). Retrieved from https://www.academia .edu/1106536/Online_Teaching_and_Classroom_Change_the_Trans-Classroom _Teacher_in_the_Age_of_the_Internet

Novak, G., Patterson, E., Gavrin, A., & Christian, W. (1999). *Just-in-time teaching: Blending active learning with web technology.* Upper Saddle River, NJ: Prentice Hall.

Scherff, L., Singer, N. R., & Brown, A. (2013). Mentoring "pre" preservice teachers in third spaces. *Teacher Education and Practice, 26*(3), 375–392.

Short, J., Williams, E., & Christie, B. (1976). *The social psychology of telecommunications.* Hoboken, NJ: John Wiley & Sons.

Shulman, L. S. (1987). Knowledge and teaching: Foundations of the new reform. *Harvard Educational Review, 57*(1), 1–23.

Siemens, G. (2004, December 12). Connectivism: A learning theory for the digital age. Retrieved from http://www.ingedewaard.net/papers/Connectivism/2005_siemens _ALearning TheoryForTheDigitalAge.pdf

Turner, V. (1975). *Dramas, fields, and metaphors: Symbolic action in human society.* Ithaca, NY: Cornell University Press.

Van Manen, M. (1977). Linking ways of knowing with ways of being practical. *Curriculum Inquiry, 6,* 205–228.

Applications and Software Referenced

Adobe Acrobat is software for creating, modifying, and reading files in the portable document format (PDF). It is available as free version with reader-only capabilities or for a monthly subscription as a full version (https://acrobat.adobe.com/us/en/; now Adobe Acrobat DC; Chapter 3).

Adobe Breeze is now a component of Adobe Connect (see below; Chapter 2).

Adobe Connect is a web conferencing application that is widely used for small group collaboration, virtual classrooms, and large scale webinars. This application allows multiple break-out sessions for small group collaborations and convenient recording of online meetings for those later viewing. Mobile app is available for smartphone users (http://www.adobe.com/products/adobeconnect.html; Chapters 3 & 6).

BigBlueButton is an open-source online web-conferencing platform that is free for all. It includes video, audio, and text-based communication, a wide board, and the option to record a meeting to view later (http://bigbluebutton.org; Chapter 6).

Blackboard is a learning management system. It is used to design and deliver e-learning and includes many specific products, such as Elluminate, listed below (http://www .blackboard.com/; Chapter 3).

Blackboard Elluminate offers advanced virtual classroom technology for synchronous live courses over the web (sas.elluminate.com; Chapter 7).

Blog.com is a website that offers free blog space (www.blog.com; Chapter 7).

Canvas is a learning management system used to design and deliver e-learning (http:// www.instructure.com/; Chapter 3).

Co:writer is an application that uses vocabulary and grammar cues to predict the words that users will need but might not know. It can be used on desktop computers as well as a host of portable devices (http://donjohnston.com/cowriter; Chapter 3).

Diigo is a social bookmarking site where users may store and organize links to other websites and see the links stored by other users (http://www.diigo.com; Chapter 4).

Dragon NaturallySpeaking is dictation software for home and professional use (http://www.nuance.com/dragon/index.htm; Chapter 3).

Facebook is a social networking application where users may become "friends" with other users in order to share text, photo, and video posts as well as private messages. Originally Facebook required a .edu e-mail username, restricting its target market to college students or graduates. However, that limitation is no longer in place, allowing the application a much wider range. It can be used on desktop computers as well as numerous portable devices (http://www.facebook.com; Chapter 4).

Feedly is a rich site summary (RSS) feed aggregator that allows users to funnel multiple online sources into one site (http://feedly.com/index.html#welcome; Chapter 4).

Glogster is an application that allows users to combine images, text, video, audio, and other graphics to create a "multimedia interactive poster"—that is, a glog. Glogster also maintains the Glogpedia Content Library, which includes educational glogs organized by category and available for classroom use (http://edu.glogster.com/?ref=com; Chapter 3).

Google Hangouts is a communication platform offered by Google that includes instant messaging, video chat, and Internet phone features (hangouts.google.com; Chapter 2, 6, & 7).

Google Sites, a part of Google Apps, makes website creation simple (sites.google.com; Chapter 7).

HeyTell is a voice messaging app for phones, which allows users to send audio messages to one another (http://heytell.com/front.html; Chapter 2).

Hubspot is a website that offers free blog space (www.hubspot.com; Chapter 7).

KakaoTalk is a messaging application that allows users to send texts, videos, photos, and other media (subject to standard text messaging rates). It can be used on desktop computers as well as numerous portable devices (http://www.kakao.com/talk; Chapter 2).

Kaltura includes a number of video publishing products that allow users to integrate videos into their learning management systems. (http://corp.kaltura.com/; Chapter 3).

Kurzweil 1000 is a scanning and reading software that converts text into speech and allows users to customize the listening experience by changing the speed, pitch, and emphasis (https://www.kurzweiledu.com/products/kurzweil-1000-v14-windows.html; Chapter 3).

Magnoto is a blog and website building application that features easily changeable templates and formats (http://www.magnoto.com/; Chapter 3).

MySpace is a social networking application where users may become "friends" with other users in order to share text, photo, and video posts as well as private messages. It most often used as a way for musicians, bands, filmmakers, and other artists to connect with fans (http://www.myspace.com; Chapter 4).

Netvibes is a rich site summary (RSS) feed aggregator that allows users to funnel multiple online sources into one site (http://www.netvibes.com/en; Chapter 4).

Nota includes applications for creating slideshows and notes (http://www.notainc.com; Chapter 3).

Oncourse is a learning management system for students and faculty at Indiana University used to design and deliver e-learning (https://oncourse.iu.edu/portal; Chapter 3).

PB Works provides a variety of collaboration products, including space for collaborative wikis (www.pbworks.com; Chapter 7).

Pinterest is a social bookmarking site where users may store and organize links to other websites and see the links stored by other users (https://www.pinterest.com/; Chapter 4).

PowerPoint is presentation software from the Microsoft Office Suite (http://www .microsoftstore.com; Chapter 3).

Quandary is an application for creating Web-based educational mazes (http://www .halfbakedsoftware.com/quandary.php; Chapter 2).

ScrapBlog is an application for creating an online scrapbooks containing photos, videos, and audio (https://www.crunchbase.com/organization/scrapblog; Chapter 3).

Skype is a widely used online service for video and voice chat as well as instant messaging (www.skype.com; Chapter 2 & 7).

Storybird is an application that allows users to create books using their own text, graphics, and Storybird's cache of graphics and illustrations (https://storybird.com/; Chapter 3).

Symbaloo is a social bookmarking site where users may store and organize links to other websites and see the links stored by other users (http://www.symbaloo.com/home /mix/13eOcK1fiV; Chapter 4).

Tango is a free messaging, video, and voice application for handheld tablets and phones. It allows users to share photos, music, play games, and communicate over Wi-Fi or subject to standard rates (http://www.tango.me/; Chapter 2).

TeacherTube is a secure, accessible, and free space for sharing student-created videos (www.teachertube.com; Chapter 3).

Twitter is a social networking site where users communicate with 140-character messages called "tweets" (http://www.twitter.com; Chapter 1 & 4).

Voice Thread is a collaborative presentation application that supports photos, videos, and voice recordings (http://www.voicethread.com; Chapter 2).

WhatsApp is an application that uses cellular data to support its non-SMS messaging (https://www.whatsapp.com/; Chapter 2).

Wikidot is space for building wiki-based websites (www.wikidot.com; Chapter 7).

Wikispaces is a social writing platform for education. It is free for teachers and students. Wikispaces now has over 10 million registered educators and students on the platform (www.wikispaces.com; Chapter 7).

WordPress is a website that offers free space for personal blogs and business sites (www.wordpress.com; Chapter 7).

Zoom Text is magnification and reading software for users with limited or no vision (http://www.zoomtext.com/products/zoomtext-magnifierreader/; Chapter 3).